Dean Carey is an intelligent and creative teacher and theatre person; his rapport with his students is marvellous.

Robert Benedetti, California Institute of the Arts

Full of such essential truth that it seems at once revelatory and confirmatory. This book will give the actor a massive injection of self-confidence at the same time propelling them into unknown territory. An affirmation of the actor's great strength – instinct. Buy it!

Hugo Weaving, Actor

Surely the final journey for the actor is the personal, the exploration of the instinct – 'to be as good as *I* can be'. At last a book to help me on my way.

Marcus Graham, Actor

This book is filled with catalysts to fire your imagination, expand your awareness and galvanise your will. Buy this book and you will never work alone again!

Lindy Davies, Theatre Director

This book is a 'must read' for any actor facing auditions, not only because it is practical, helpful and full of good ideas, but because Dean's entertaining examples and inspiring insight unite us all in a common love for the work and an aspiration to do our very best.

Gale Edwards, Theatre Director

For auditionees and performers interested in an intelligent and insightful analysis of the state of theatrical practice, this book is essential and profitable reading.

Wayne Harrison, Director, Sydney Theatre Company

Masterclass revitalises all those basic acting impulses you keep forgetting, with a precision, ease and common sense that is stimulating and reassuring. A masterful work.

John Bell, The Bell Shakespeare Company

Dean's book stokes the seers within, it reminds us why we are actors. It is universally valuable to me – whether I am auditioning in Sydney, New York or LA.

Gia Carides, Actor

DEAN CAREY has been involved extensively in theatrical education for over 14 years. He has taught for the AFTRS, the Nimrod Company, Belvoir Street Theatre and the NSW Conservatorium. He taught at NIDA for five years and was Associate Head of Acting. He was then appointed Head of Acting at the WA Academy of Performing Arts where, over his four-year stay, he directed *A Month in the Country, Peer Gynt, Dark of the Moon, Flora the Red Menace, The Rover* and *The Golden Age*. He also directed *Savage Love, The Touch of Silk, Late Arrivals, Sunrise, Children of the Sun* and *Tales From the Vienna Woods*.

He has conducted guest workshops throughout the US at the University of California in San Diego, CalArts and the University of Southern California in Los Angeles, The American Conservatory Theatre in San Francisco, Ensemble Theatre Company in Florida and the Los Angeles High School of Performing Arts. Dean also works as a dialogue coach and performance consultant in the film and television industries.

In 1986 he established The Actor's Centre in Sydney, a professional development base for industry workers and students of acting. Its charter was, and still is, to facilitate the extension of essential skills and to enhance the performer's productivity.

In that same year his first book, *The Actor's Audition Manual*, was published by Currency Press and has since sold over 12,000 copies.

MASTERCLASS

THE ACTOR'S AUDITION MANUAL

MEN

Dean Carey

NICK HERN BOOKS
London

First published in Great Britain 1995
by Nick Hern Books Limited,
14 Larden Road, London W3 7ST
by arrangement with Currency Press, Australia

A CIP catalogue record for this book is available
from the British Library.

ISBN 1 85459 238 6 (Women)
ISBN 1 85459 233 5 (Men)

Typeset by Currency and The Master Typographer
Printed in Australia by Southwood Press, Sydney, NSW
Cover design by Anaconda Graphic Design

Preface

This book is a companion to *The Actor's Audition Manual,* first published in 1985. In Part One of this book you will find important updates on the art of auditioning, as well as fresh information to help re-direct your energies and allow maximum benefit from every audition opportunity.

In Part Two, using speeches as examples, we'll explore in detail a range of exercises which may challenge the way you work on your piece. A number of powerful and *practical* ways are fully illustrated, which aim to release the speech's dynamic range and increase your sense of personal ownership. They will prove an invaluable stimulus and resource when rehearsing and preparing. They will energise your approach and encourage your creative drive.

In Part Three you will find a collection of around one hundred monologues for theatre auditions *and* film and television screen tests. Many actors are now being asked to present rehearsed pieces for screen tests, and some of the speeches in Part Three have been selected especially for this environment. Collected over the last seven years, these monologues present a wide range of exciting possibilities for you to practise your art.

I thank the countless number of actors who, through their commitment and courage in my workshops, have helped design and develop the exercises in this book to their present form. I am sure your work will benefit as a result and you will fulfil your desire to discover more about the craft, that leads toward the art.

Dean Carey, Sydney 1995

Copyright Acknowledgments

Acknowledgments

I would like to sincerely thank Dr. Geoffrey Gibbs and all his staff at the Western Australia Academy of Performing Arts – particularly Lisle Jones. His intimate knowledge of the craft of acting and the passion it takes to be an artist has helped to establish WAAPA as one of the leading national acting institutions. I have felt privileged to be associated with a disciplined and nurturing educational facility which produces students whose attitude and approach to the industry is respected by all professionals.

Many thanks are due to my research assistant, Mary-Anne Gifford, whose tireless efforts culminated in the collating of over five hundred speeches in over 110 degree heat.

Thanks yet again to the staff at the NIDA library for their assistance and welcome support.

Both the Performing Arts and Ariel Bookshops in Sydney also offered their guidance and help.

Finally, thankyou to the following people for their encouragement and advice; Bob Griffiths, Tony Knight, Chris Edmund, Glenn B. Swift, Monique Spanbrook, and Lisa Schouw.

Photographic Credits

PLATE 1 Photo: Jon Green; Actor: Lisa Baumwol • PLATE 2 Photo: Jon Green; Actor: Roxane Wilson • PLATE 3 Photo: Terry Smith; Actor: Heidi Lapaine • PLATE 4 Photo: Eric Sierins; Actors: John Adam & Deborah Galanos • PLATE 5 Photo: Jon Green; Actors: Hugh Jackson & Dean Carey • PLATE 6 Photo: Jon Green; Actors: Jennifer Botica & Dean Carey • PLATE 7 Photo: Jon Green; Actors: Jennifer Botica & Dean Carey • PLATE 8 Photo: Terry Smith; Actors: Journey Students • PLATE 9 Photo: Jon Green; Actors: (*l.* to *r.*) Simon Lyndon, Lisa Baumwol, Wadih Dona, Lucille Reynolds, Ben Harkin, Marin Mimica, Natasha McNamara, Dominic Purcell • PLATE 10 Photo: Branco Gaica; Actors: Lisa Bailey and Damian Pike.

PART ONE

The Path
to Process

Chapter 1

Road Testing

The Bottom Line

You have an audition coming up. Yes, you will have to *act*. There's no doubt about it. You might chat for a while, discuss future projects, speak of your 'life in art' but, at some stage without fail, they're going to say, 'Act!'.

Unfortunately, unlike other creative artists, you have chosen an art form which will not be satisfied with a piece of pottery, a painting on canvas, a sequenced sound or a stone sculpture to allow its release. It uses *you*. *You* are its vehicle. You can't create wildly in the privacy of your own home — trying, testing, experimenting — then after completion, send off the demo tape or invite the prospective buyers and dealers to your gallery showing. You front up and *become* your own product.

All things being equal, the audition may go well and be very acceptable. Your personal 'product launch' may have been charming, skilful and efficient, proving yet again your ability to understand what was required and as a result, deliver the goods. But did your selection resonate with your stamp of truth? Did it speak in ways which *revealed* you? Was it a personal statement affecting *change* within you and those watching?

The Authentic Self

We all want our work to resound with our uniqueness. What then prohibits or inhibits this from happening? Jacques Copeau, one of France's most prolific actors, directors and theatricians, strode into his office at the Theatre du Vieux Colombier after directing a rehearsal, frustrated and at a crossroad:

> Did you see them again today? I always know in advance what they are going to do. They cannot get out of themselves. They reduce

3

everything to the level of their own habits, their cliches, their affectations. They do not invent anything. It is all sheer imitation of imitation. [1]

Why do we succumb to this imitation? So often it seems our focus falls on *trying to get it right* — we attempt to present a suitable form which will 'read' as appropriate to those viewing. We deliver a set of polished and efficient acting 'signals' to successfully demonstrate our ability and talent. This accent on form can be extremely lethal to our sense of invention and our instinctive personal investment.

Our strong need to get it right, to do what will be acceptable, to have the correct vocal and physical qualities in order that the work be seen as 'valid', compounds this imitation. Once there, our uniqueness deserts us and is replaced by a highly polished exterior or shell, encasing what we have created and leaving our performance bereft of its pure interior truth.

After an exercise I often ask the actors to state, on a scale of one to ten, how *correct* they were aiming to be. Many say between seven and ten. I then ask, on the same scale, 'How active was your *instinct*?' The answer is often 'three'. The reason? The actors were focusing once again on trying to achieve what they believed were *my* wishes or the results *I* was looking for. As a result, imitation emerges and the authentic self is silenced.

I then ask the actors what could they do to allow their level three instinct to be *doubled*? After a few searching moments where they reorder their priorities, they answer: 'Forget about you... follow my impulses... physicalise more'. We then repeat the scene. This time the actors' attention rests firmly on the precise and accurate directions they have given themselves. Consequently, their work departs from the world of imitation, from 'this is what it *would* be like *if* I was feeling...' to 'this is what it *is* like to feel...'.

The work speaks with much more individuality as the actors develop a reality based on their *instincts* and *honesty*. The learning that results becomes far more valuable to the actors because it has been *their* discovery and clarification of *their* individual processes. For acting cannot be taught, only learnt.

My task as a teacher is to provide the most potent opportunities in which actors can become more intimate with their creative process — what undermines and thwarts it, what affirms and accelerates it. I believe *this* to be the most effective contribution I can make to each developing artist.

In summary, there are two distinct modes actors work within — one is the *inventing* mode, where they aim to please and impress, the other is the *responding* mode, where they allow themselves to react and experience. If an actor is working to invent, I often ask them to do the first eight lines of the scene where their sole focus is to please *me*. Then we repeat the first eight lines with the sole focus being to please *themselves*. I then ask which feels more effective? The key is to work towards self-satisfaction through creative autonomy.

The Court is Now in Session

One reason actors lose their self-trust and become separated from their inner 'hunch' is that many believe the teacher knows how it should be played and that they don't. It's very necessary for every actor to realise that the teacher, and indeed director, often *doesn't know* how the scene should look, sound and feel. All they are sure about is that the potent cocktail of circumstances surrounding the characters should promote a series of dynamic exchanges. As the actors react to these circumstances, so does the director. Then together the cast and director edit and craft these various choices of reaction, to eventually produce meaning — the production's *vision*.

With the belief that the person out front 'knows it all', the actor's job becomes more of a trial — a series of long days second-guessing and end-gaining in order to validate their casting and eventually, their self-worth. Once you release yourselves from this crippling approach, rehearsals become an expedition where creative discovery and fulfilment once again become possible.

The entire thrust of my teaching over the past twelve years has been towards unearthing ways of releasing the actor from the *limits* of imitation. By offering you the opportunity to connect with the purity of the work, it is hoped that you may ultimately replace product with *process*, results with *evolution* and predetermining with *perception*.

The exercises in this book are therefore designed to:
• activate an organic, physical life
• promote deep personal connections
• extend the boundaries of your unique expression.

This book will offer active and potent ways to enable you to shed the sense of 'correctness' which many actors aim for, so that your instinctive and intuitive self may achieve full disclosure through your work. We will also look closely at structure, function, playwright's intention, and what Stanislavsky called the actor's *score*. Without this score, you're relying on luck and 'feeling right' on the night. Danger! We all know that the purity and permission we *privately* allow ourselves can be robbed from us by anything which makes us feel self-conscious. In an audition there are countless dynamics around us which, if plugged into, will lead us quite successfully to feeling nothing *but* self-conscious. As you will see in the chapters ahead, the actor's score carefully crafts each moment in order to establish a confident and solid knowledge of the inner workings of the character and the surrounding scene. As Stanislavsky said:

the artist... must be the master of his own inspiration and must know how to call it forth at the hour announced on the posters of the theatre. This is the chief secret of our art.[2]

To Repeat or Not to Repeat

The actor's job is twofold — to be capable of *repeating* every moment and to be able to *justify* all action.

Without the score of your scene — the precise plotting of the character's moment-by-moment journey — you run the enormous risk of being a legend in your lounge room, but feeling a non-entity in the audition room.

Inspiration comes and goes – adrenalin can get you through, but quickly fades with constant use...

Technique and skill can ensure *accurate repetition* and therefore *re-creation*.

Technique without instinct is hollow. Instinct without technique is blind.[3]

Your score defines your work and gives your instinct the foundation from which to fly.

In Part Two, The Creative Arena, we will look at audition speeches and uncover their scores. This will provide a solid base from which you can activate your instinctive powers.

The Job of Justifying

The audience needs to see *reasons* for the character's actions. The actor must then *own* these reasons sufficiently so as to allow the actions, thoughts and emotions to spring from this inner source.

Let's take an imaginary scene: Man One runs onto the stage, shouts, leaps for joy, and yells 'Life is fine!' Woman One enters wielding a chainsaw, cuts out his heart and screams 'Revenge!'. Blackout.

Not a play I'd particularly stand in line to see, but in order to act Man One, you must justify it all — the run, the leap, the choice of words and all the circumstances prior to his entry. These may include six years of marriage leading to divorce, the guilt, turmoil and anguish of leaving his wife, his eventual escape to a tropical hide-out and now, the imminent and long-awaited arrival of his new lover. He may finally feel, for the first time in his life, that all is at last well, and life is indeed 'fine'.

Ownership

You not only have to justify but you must *personalise* each circumstance. You must create personal *connections* to every word, idea, action, emotion and gesture your character inhabits if you're to create a vivid and defined stage life.

An actor friend went for a role in an episode of the TV series *A Country Practice*. The character description was 'distraught mother': she had lost her child through cot death. As a result of her distress she had fainted and split open her head. We see her in the casualty area of the local hospital — obviously 'distraught' and in great pain and shock. She is attended to with care and understanding by the doctor and a number of nurses who admit her for observation overnight. The next morning the doctor arrives by her bedside and asks 'And how are you today?' She replies, 'Better — I feel slightly better this morning... (taking the doctor's hand) thankyou'.

To say that one line in your performance you may have to imaginatively connect to, and therefore personalise, the following: the first time you met your husband, the first date, the decision to marry, moving into the house, discovery of the pregnancy, painting the nursery, hanging the mobiles above the cot, the trauma and elation of giving birth, the first touch of the child's skin, the first look into its eyes, leaving hospital with the child, tucking it into its new bed, the newness and special quality of that first week, and then finally, the devastating and horrific pre-dawn discovery of the baby's death.

You'll be asked to act many situations which you have never had any experience of. This is where you enter the world of the imagined — Stanislavsky's 'magic if'. *If* I lived in the same circumstance as the character, *if* I had the same background, age, social status, outlook, and *if* these events happened to me, how would *I* feel, think, react?

'If' acts as a lever to lift us out of the world of actuality and into the realm of the imagination.[4]

It is within this world that secret and hidden truths lie. We as actors have access to this world and because of this, our art can flourish.

This imaginative exploration becomes the springboard to our onstage reality. Our words, actions, ideas and emotions begin as imagined, for they are not our own. But the journey is one of claiming them, decoding them, embracing them and then lastly being transformed by them. This is often called 'grounding' the work.

To help form this essential foundation it is wise to start from the nucleus of truth within you: *you* are a human being, so too is your character. Therefore, there must be parts of the character and yourself which cross over. To pinpoint this mutual emotional fibre, ask what universal *wants* you share with your character: control, survival, power, freedom, love, respect. Allow these elemental human needs to connect the emotions of the play to your own. In short, you hook up to the forces driving the character and in turn create an emotional fusion between their world and your own.

The *process* of personalisation differs greatly from actor to actor. Some prefer to imagine in minute detail every aspect of the character's situation. With appropriate music as an underscore, they might lie on the floor and run an imaginary film through their head — emotionally exploring and subsequently investing each and every frame with meaning and consequence.

Others write letters or poetry as if from the character's hand. This process of articulating on paper the precise interior state and perspective of the character allows the actor to understand the human cost and emotional significance of each moment.

Talking to people who have experienced or witnessed the exact or similar circumstances can be a key and major stimulus for the actor. Artworks, films, novels, journals, sculpture, music — all of these can transport you from the world of actuality and into the realm of your imagination. They can fuse the actor's and character's connection to the situation. This then particularises, humanises and *personalises* each dynamic thread which, when woven together, reveal the character in relation to their world.

Remember: Approaches such as these and the many exercises in the chapters to follow are designed to be used *if* instinct isn't enough. Techniques are there to support, not replace, instinct. You must keep reminding yourselves of this. Trust in your inner hunch — be courageous and follow your initial impulses and instincts. If necessary, use techniques as triggers, as strategies. 'The first aspect of the method (any method) is to get the unconscious to work. The second is, once it starts, to leave it alone.' [5]

Naturally

For whatever reason, you may be able to play the role with ease — justifying all behaviour and connecting to the feelings behind the dialogue *instantly*. Sometimes we 'know' the material, we intuitively feel we could play this role. So, 'if it 'ain't broke, don't fix it'.

But if it isn't exactly broken but it's also not state of the art, then some personal exploration of the interior landscape of the character becomes vital. For a one-line moment in a television episode I wouldn't suggest weeks of research and living-in at your local hospital. But some specific work to stimulate the imagination and help claim the material may prove to be invaluable. Through your ability to fill in and flesh out every detail you start to become physically and emotionally *transformed*. To allow this transformation to take place you must essentially have ownership of the character's circumstances and their world. Ultimately, this requires a *personal investment* on your behalf.

Exposure

Some actors fear the 'exposure' of some part of themselves. They fear that the pain or joy or hatred of their character may be misinterpreted as *them* releasing some part of *their* inner feelings. This concern stifles and inhibits many actors and robs them of the wealth of human experience within them. It leads them to abandon their authentic self and to act through the imitation discussed earlier.

In a class, rehearsal or audition you may reveal quite strong and deep personal feelings or connections to the material. Quite powerful resonances may be felt as a result of the collision (or indeed collusion) between the material and yourself. But this personal

9

exposure need never concern you. Why? Because, as Lisle Jones once said in a class at the Academy, the audience will *never know* — they will only ever think it's good acting.

Student actors can also feel threatened by the demands of the work. The intense expectation to 'reveal' or to 'risk' can be daunting. I once heard it said that actors are actors because their souls are close to the surface. There is truth in this. There are times when the character's pain is your pain, his or her fears, yours. Relax in the knowledge that you have a full-time safety net — people are looking for, and hoping to see, good acting.

When your work resonates due to your personal attachments and the atmosphere which surrounds you becomes charged through your personal exposure, your acting becomes *informed*. Those watching will applaud your *craft*, regardless of where it may have been forged.

In the following chapter we will look at the nature of the creative process and discuss ways to engage these personal links in all we do.

Chapter 2

The Creative State

The Secret Fear

'All right', I hear you say, 'what if I create from my *authentic self*, I expose my truth informed by the very depth of my imagination, and... it doesn't work? People don't applaud the event. The risk *doesn't* pay off. I *don't* get the job!!!' You may think perhaps, it's better to simply imitate the appropriate and remain safe, rather than sorry. This approach can be seductive and, when fuelled by fear, can greatly undermine your true creative potential.

We certainly haven't chosen an easy task and in our art form there are no sure solutions. We are throwing our hat into the ring every time we perform.

So often in interviews with internationally acclaimed artists you hear them express the same fear — that *this* time they'll be found out for sure! Somehow the next project will expose them as an impostor and a fraud. They'll be publicly humiliated then ostracised for all eternity. Even though things may have been going *quite* well for *quite* some time with, dare I say, *quite* an amount of success, *this* time, all will be revealed in a blaze of embarrassing mediocrity.

And why shouldn't you feel this? Every job or task you undertake is unique — a one-off. Just when you get the hang of a role, the season closes and you find yourself thrust into another alien situation where nothing is tangible and all is at stake and at risk... again. A new play, new actors, a new director, a different vision to follow, a new life form for you to make real so that within five or so weeks of rehearsal, it will walk and talk and people won't run screaming from the theatre! The only common thread that is woven through this succession of challenges is that very familiar fear — *this* time, it could all go wrong.

What can be said? It's part of the terrain. It comes with the territory. Every artist feels it, to a greater or lesser extent, constantly. If you *didn't*, then what would your art consist of? It would be safe, perhaps smug, self-content. It would be without risk, self-investment, personal

11

truth. Would you wish to be in a profession which *didn't* embrace these qualities?

The Courage to Create

In his book entitled *Creativity*, C.R. Rogers talks about the internal opposites at work during the creative process. The first is what he calls the 'Eureka feeling: 'This is *it*!'; 'I have discovered!'; 'This is what I wanted to express!'.

The second he calls 'the anxiety of separateness'. He explains that he does not believe that many significant creative products are formed without the feelings: 'I am alone. No one has ever done just this before. I have ventured into territory where no one has been. Perhaps I am foolish, or wrong, or lost, or abnormal'.

So you're in good company! During the creative process we *all* feel this inner friction. But we continue nevertheless. Through this internal turmoil, where foolishness and chaos abide, our need to externalise ourselves through a creative statement prevails. Some say that art is the search for clarity and resolution. For many of us this search is ongoing.

The next challenge to our inner belief is a *post*-creative one: how, *after* we create, do we *evaluate* our work? What do we focus upon when everyone around us has their definitive opinion and exacting personal taste?

Perhaps the most fundamental condition of creativity is that the source of evaluative judgment is internal. The value of the product is, for the creative person, established not by the praise or criticism of others, but by ourselves. Have I created something satisfying to *me*? Does it express part of me — my feeling or my thought, my pain or my ecstasy? These are the only questions which really matter to the creative person.

This does not mean that we are oblivious to, or unwilling to be aware of, the judgment of others. It is simply that the basis of evaluation lies within ourself, in our own organismic reaction to and appraisal of our product. If to the person it has the 'feel' of being 'me in action', of being an actualisation of potentialities in ourself which heretofore have not existed and are now emerging into existence, then it is satisfying and creative, and no outside evaluation can change that fundamental fact.[6]

Only with this attitude can you forge ahead, continuing your quest for creative expression through affirming the partnership between who you are and what you create.

Archaeological

Leaving aside external criticism or praise (for some of us, this is the easiest input to place in perspective), what happens if *you* believe your work and effort wasn't a true reflection of your potential? For whatever reason, *you* were unsatisfied?

Firstly, you must acknowledge that once you've created something — presented your audition, which is an act of creation — that creation is finished. It has been completed. For what you created was only a reflection of where you were at, at that exact moment in your life. It was a point in the process. If your creative process is to *continue* you must now move on, allowing your ever-growing knowledge and perception to inform your work. Otherwise you can become anchored to that moment — a creative history repeating itself and producing a cycle lacking in freshness and naivety.

I once saw a production called *Archaeological* at the Sydney Performance Space, in which one of the performers had designed, constructed and then played his own instruments. He stood in a tight, overhead smoky spotlight and raised a small and beautifully crafted clay pipe to his lips. From the silence came a delicate and haunting sound. The very air surrounding him seemed to vibrate.

After the last long note gently faded, he took the pipe from his lips, raised it up as if in reverence, then allowed it to slip from his fingers and shatter on the floor below. His creative gesture had served its purpose. He now moved on to craft another vehicle in which to channel his creative impulse.

The same is true of your work. Some actors hold onto past 'failures' (and sometimes successes) and become doomed to repeat the pattern by not approaching each new task with freshness and genuine spontaneity. The act of creation must be a response to where you are at as a person at that time. The sum of your personal energies and life-force at that instant in your life produces a play, a poem, a piece of pottery, a role in a production. As you move through your work, you grow, develop and change. This is unavoidable. Your creative gestures *will* be renewed by this journey *if* you embrace each step and give yourselves the courage and the *permission* to keep creating.

In other words, the adventure continues...

Original Sin

> Creativity is the surrender of the infinite possibilities on the altar of form.[7]

In a sense, this may be true. But each time we work we face the thrill and challenge of playing with, and losing ourselves in, the infinite possibilities *without* being bound by a preconceived idea of the form our creativity should ultimately take. Obviously there will come a time when the choices we have made must be justified in terms of serving the story and fulfilling what we believe to be the playwright's intentions.

Initially however, what do you need to focus on... being creative?, clever?, original?, unique? Unfortunately, striving for these qualities can easily condemn an actor to a miserable life of repetition. In our often manic and vain attempt to be 'original' we focus on what has worked in the past or what we 'once saw', which may now be applicable if repeated. We then regurgitate old patterns within patterns, creating imitation upon imitation.

Remember — you are the only person in the world who looks like you and has had the same background, upbringing, education, cultural conditioning and experiences. How much more original do you want to be? Therefore, attempting to be 'creative' can easily lead to a focus on form rather than on content, and can stifle the ease with which you wish to work. Only by surrendering your need to know what may happen, how your piece should look and sound, and by following your organic impulses, will a free exploration and a pure creative release occur. Remember: process not product; content over form.

Basically, you have two choices: to *act* based on what you've seen or done before, or to *react* based on what you think and feel *now*. The hardest thing can be to get some actors to stop worrying and controlling what they think *should* happen, and to surrender and experience what *is* happening.

Part Two of this book offers a host of opportunities to launch your imagination, based on what you *think* and *feel* — in essence, reconnecting to your authentic self.

Permission to Play

A useful strategy to avoid the burden of trying to be original is to find ways of enabling yourself to toy with elements and concepts instead of having a fixed attitude about what you wish to achieve:

> Associated with the openness and lack of rigidity... is the ability to
> play spontaneously with ideas, colours, shapes, relationships — to
> juggle elements into impossible juxtapositions, to shape wild hypo-
> theses, to make the given problematic, to express the ridiculous, to
> translate from one form to another... it is from this spontaneous
> toying and exploration that there arises the hunch, the creative
> seeing of life in a new and significant way. It is as though out of the
> wasteful spawning of thousands of possibilities there emerges one
> or two evolutionary forms with the qualities which give them a
> more permanent value.[8]

So to create freely you must give yourselves the *permission to play*.
You must release your grip on form and shape and enter the arena of
'what could be'. From this vantage point, your invention can become
limitless.

The Essential Source
In 1991 I had the privilege of teaching at the truly extraordinary
Shchukin Higher Theatre School of the Vakhtangov State Academic
Theatre in Moscow. It was to be a remarkable experience.

The ride from the airport was just as I had imagined: scenes of
bleakness, desolation and aimlessness, as if all the colour had drained
from the sky, land and people; incredible sights of huge, stolid towers
of flats — all grey, uniform, certain and strong, yet dilapidated and on
the verge of decay. Sounds of gunshots became fireworks as the city
celebrated Anti-Aircraft Day. I stood by the Moscow River in the
bitter cold to witness this synchronised display launched from over
twenty locations — organised, precise, constrained. As the night sky
exploded all around it was as if a brutal war had begun without
warning. Then, just as abruptly, the sky dissolved into flames of
orange and smoke.

This was certainly a welcome beyond any other. What was I to
expect from the actors?! A fierce grip on form and product? A
technical rigidity? Too much command and control over their energy
as a result of their strict discipline? What would they make of *my*
work?

The building the class took place in was more like an old ballroom
— crumbling, raw, full of history. We climbed the fourteen sets of

stairs and entered the rehearsal room on the top floor. With my translator at the ready, I mustered my forces and began the class.

I was right: they *were* technical masters of their bodies which are their instruments, accurate and precise. But their skills were matched with another passionate belief: they knew in their minds and hearts that the process towards creation relies on *risk*, *daring* and *courage*. This knowledge manifested itself in *sensory* and *kinaesthetic* (physical) connections. For them, it was the vital foundation for the acting journey. Their bodies became vessels from which their spirits were able to take flight. These Russian actors were impassioned and totally committed. It was an absolute joy to work with them. They demonstrated such clarity, inner concentration, and a vigorous freedom of expression. They knew that all of their painstaking, back-breaking, mechanical and technical classes would produce *skills*, which would release and support their creativity, and without this work, their inspiration would be flawed.

Many of the exercises in this book were workshopped in that class. The actors' excitement grew as they could feel the energy associated with the exercises begin to effect their muscles. I believe that it is at *this* level that deep learning takes place. Ultimately, these actors had been taught (or had been allowed to learn) that instinct and intuition, once given permission, will lead to authentic personal creation.

How then can we activate this permission? Where does it reside?

The Creative State

It has been said that the acting craft can be separated into three main elements: *intuition*, *imagination*, *common sense*. To me these elements represent the following:

Intuition is often called the actor's 'hunch'; the instinct within that provides the actor with creative impulses born of his or her inner, unspoken knowledge. It can vary in response to the material you work on. Your intuitive connections may sometimes be fierce, yet at other times this inner knowledge eludes you and you must look elsewhere to support your creative drive.

Common sense concerns itself with what is known, or the facts. For example, your craft and technical knowledge may offer logical solutions to any acting demand. This is guided by what you believe or know to be the playwright's intentions. Common sense enables you to employ any element of technique which you believe will help in the achievement of your acting goal.

Imagination encompasses your appetite for all that is possible. In this interior 'dream state' you allow yourself the licence to explore each idea with an unlimited scope. Logical boundaries, preconceived parameters and the sense of the appropriate, desert you. You find yourself dissolving the lifeline to the 'parent ship' and, with courage and naivety, following your fantasy.

It is in *this* state that your inner critic is set aside. The fax in your head awaiting reception lies idle. The usual incoming messages — *You cannot do this... It can't be done... You're going to be wrong... What you're attempting is not within your range...Give up now before you're worthlessness becomes too evident... Stick to what you know... stay safe, otherwise, you'll only get hurt* — these commands do not compute. You find no program with which to access them. But inwardly you observe one lone signal, gently blinking: *I'm right with you... where shall we go?*

At these moments everything seems easy. Any challenge empowers you. Your child-like innocence and playfulness runs in tandem with your extraordinary wealth of human experience and, out of this, you begin to actualise your potential. Without attempting to be original, *this* is where your uniqueness resides.

Concepts Made Concrete

Much of my teaching has been an exploration and indeed affirmation of the actor's 'creative state'. I have, with my actors, continued to discover how this state may be induced and what obstacles emerge to thwart it. Through various structures used as launching pads, it has been our aim to activate the physical radiation of one's *aliveness*, hence allowing the pure, unadulterated release of the actor's *free child*, where the creative spirit resides.

All of the exercises are aimed at getting the focus off you and onto the other actor and your shared moment-by-moment stage life. They are about *activation:* igniting the actor's *interior fire*; making active all the dynamics you will require on the rehearsal room floor and in performance — aliveness, receptivity, communication, contact, the here and now, passion, courage, versatility, open channels, inventiveness, surrender, vulnerability, joy, power, alertness, sensory awareness — in essence, activating the creative, authentic self.

There is one aspect of my work which I actually call 'Creative State'. These classes are usually non-verbal and involve the entire class for the duration of the session. They are mostly highly energetic and eccentric, but are sometimes simple, subtle and internalised. They can be extremely rhythmic, patterned and conceptual, but they always release and support the actor's imagination and creative drive. For a product is never sought, a judgment never made.

As a result the actors feel affirmed and any blocks or barriers often seem less permanent, for the class jettisons the actor into a world where he or she can be at one with his or her creativity and unique outlook. As such, this class becomes a 'touchstone' to each individual's sense of self and the reason he or she creates. So often drama schools focus primarily on the *success* of actors in their current production rather than on *preparing* them for their future creative lives. This lethal cocktail of 'success' mixed with 'correctness' can lead to what I call the see-I-can-do-it style of acting, which reduces creative evolution to mere pushing, proving and attaining.

Interestingly, during my first year at the Western Australian Academy of Performing Arts, I came across a book detailing the work of Michael Chekhov, a great Russian actor and teacher. He worked closely with Stanislavsky at the Moscow Art Theatre for over sixteen years and then worked around the world. Migrating to America in 1927, he established his revolutionary and much acclaimed acting studio as well as various theatre companies. He integrated the inner truth and emotional depth of Stanislavsky's system with his own sense of awakening the actor's spirit and intuition. His beliefs continued to evolve as he worked as an actor and director until his death in 1955.

In *Lessons for the Professional Actor* released in 1985, Mel Gordon's introduction states:

> Chekhov made actor-training fun. The internal censors that prevent many actors from attempting untried ideas and roles — 'not to appear stupid or ridiculous' — cease to function normally when the work is framed in a non-adult, or risk-free manner. Chekhov also created blocks of exercises that produced a rush of exhilaration or energy in his students. For Chekhov, the loss of mental energy or enthusiasm was one of the greatest obstacles to the creation of character, 'the sense of aliveness on stage'.

Coincidentally, my approach has developed along acutely similar lines: once an actor *believes* and his or her inner confidence grows, the creative state is produced. For an actor can only do something onstage if they *believe* they can. When this belief is married to an alert and heightened receptivity to the entire stage picture which surrounds them, then true shared invention becomes possible. The concept of art being a communal activity becomes a reality.

The Power Within

I remember an exhilarating class taught by the American voice specialist Rowena Balos. In this hurried lunchtime workshop, Rowena faced over sixty students from various courses and a dozen teachers, all of whom wanted to observe and take notes. But it was not to be: this was a sensory workshop. The knowledge gained was 'of the body' and would therefore be more significant in its lasting impact.

As we stood awkwardly, scattered across the rehearsal floor awaiting the commencement of the class, the room was charged with inhibition and embarrassment. A frenetic tension possessed each participant as we wondered what may be 'required' of us. Our focus was firmly anchored on what we stood to *lose*.

One of the first exercises was for all of us to stand with some space around us. Our script was, 'I am scared', and the physical movement, a sharp step *back*. After repeating this four or five times, we were asked again to repeat the line but *this* time, to step *forward*.

Why, after this exercise, was the entire room ready to freely experience all the class had to offer? Firstly, because we had acknowledged our fear and secondly, because we now stepped forward, we had replaced the unsaid word at the end of the line, 'I am scared **so** (...*I'll hold back, protect myself, stay safe*), with 'I am scared **and** (...*I'll give it a go, risk, dare to learn*).

In this state of creative openness we believe risk is rewarding, for it means growth. We know it doesn't matter *what* may happen — our focus rests securely on committing to the *process*. When this state is achieved with actors, all is indeed possible.

The next phase in Rowena's class was to step forward and replace the words 'I am scared' with 'I am powerful'! This caused a mild earth tremor when suggested. Not just 'I am scared and... *I'll give it a go*', but 'and... *I will be powerful within my creation*'. Interestingly enough, this proved a far more confronting task for the teachers than for the students. But slowly, each participant in their own way and in their own time, publicly stated there was potential for powerful creativity within them. From this point, the true process could begin.

We all know we are the source of our own creativity, our own expression. We need to be reminded and indeed encouraged to embrace that responsibility *and* open ourselves to all its possibilities.

So, to recap: '...it is from this spontaneous toying and exploration that there arises the hunch, the creative seeing of life in a new and significant way...'.

The rehearsal exercises ahead present many opportunities where you can toy with the possibilities of your *speech* and juggle *its* various elements. We will work towards unplugging from what we feel is correct and expected and surrender to our authentic connection to the purity of the work.

Chapter 3

The Basis of Craft

Pack it Up, Ship it Out

When we begin preparing for our audition, we often cannot help thinking about the presentation — we see the *form* which it might take. And why not? We want to be sure it will be perceived as legitimate and believable thereby validating our abilities.

Because we seek this validation, the first departure we often make from embracing the material in a pure way is to focus on two *end* products — *character* and *emotion*. We feel we must have these two elements alive and kicking if we're to have a chance. We imagine that if we enter these dynamic regions early in our rehearsal period we'll be truly involved and studiously *working*.

Therefore we begin involving ourselves with the package which surrounds the piece: the conditions, the state, the feelings, the sensations, how it should sound, how it should look, how it should *feel* being this other person. We are working toward *product* — towards an end result. Without adequate time spent deciphering *what* the material consists of — its structure and components — we focus on *how* it may be performed and presented. In other words, rather than *penetrating* the character's thinking, we begin to *impose* final solutions.

The danger with this approach is that it can lead to the trap discussed in Chapter One: *imitation*, that is, what you feel will be most *appropriate*. So many auditions have inadvertently foundered because of this initial approach of simply trying *too* hard *too* soon to *make it work, to get it right*.

To redress this emphasis on 'solutions' we will begin by focusing on the first stages of the process, then look at ways of channelling our creative power.

The Search for Truth

Firstly, Robert Benedetti says: 'character and emotion are not the

21

precursor of action, they are the *result* of action'. In other words, you do not have to activate these two elements to produce 'drama'. Drama springs from what happens — the events that take place, the 'action'. If in your rehearsals you *experience* this action (Stanislavsky's *score*), you will not be able to *avoid* experiencing character and emotion. They become by-products of your commitment to and fulfilment of, the scene's action.

For example, stand quite neutrally in your room with some space around you. Your script is still 'I'm scared'. Without thinking of 'how' you could say the line, or what emotion may be applicable, simply state the line whilst taking one step backwards. After doing this a couple of times, make this small adjustment: Step back a little *sharper* and with more *speed*. Whilst repeating this a few times, allow yourself to access any sensations or impulses that surface. You should sense an emotional connection beginning. Without thinking of how you *feel* or indeed *who* you are, this knowledge begins to emerge.

Now raise your arm as if you were pointing to someone. Your line is 'Stop right there'. Repeat this gesture and line three or four times. Now take a sharp step *forward* whilst swiftly raising your arm. Repeat this three or four times. Once again, the action begins to induce an attitude to what you are doing (who you are — character) and also leads to the text becoming motivated (how you feel — emotion).

The above examples are simple but hold an essential truth: Committing to the action of the scene leads to the emergence of a stronger and purer reality; working for end results can significantly retard the process towards that truth.

Looking at the greater picture for a moment, suppose your character breakdown reads: 'Bitter Old Lag'. You can't act a label, and playing a characteristic results in repetition and consistency — both hallmarks of dull acting. So what internal reasons and motivations drive the action which will *produce* this label of 'bitterness'? Through your rehearsal period you will begin to uncover the true cause — you will understand that this character is a *frustrated traditionalist*. This is the cause which results in the worldly appearance of bitterness which manifests itself in many ways and forms. The character's acute desire to have the world around them burn, given the zeal they feel for tradition, standards and principles, leads them to be constantly insulted and abused because the new world in which they find themselves thinks differently. Their actions reflect this tension: they berate, scold, contradict, defend and dismiss — bitter actions indeed.

The next role you audition for or play is labelled 'Angry Bully'. Through your internal investigation you once again form a relationship with the inner cause. Beyond the character's public persona of anger and hostility you see the *lonely, isolated searcher*. You then ensure that this is reflected in the detail of the character's exchanges — they agitate, inflame, provoke, patronise, refute and intimidate. Their anger and attitude of dominance towards all around them prevails; loneliness and isolation is set firmly within.

And so the process continues. The 'stupid eccentric' who is seen as ludicrous and often irritating, is fuelled by the *excited obsessive* within. Their actions are to demand, scrutinise, engross, indoctrinate, enthral, outsmart. They see themselves as a *visionary*, but their possessive and pedantic nature creates another impression altogether. The 'unpleasant spinster' becomes the *injured loner*, demanding emotional compensation and seeking personal validity though reproaching, demeaning and disenchanting.

When the italics supplied by the playwright before the line read '*Hysterical*', you connect to the inner stimulus which you discover to be absolute *fear*, which causes the outward signs called 'hysteria'. When the character '*violently lashes out*' you incorporate into your internal landscape the stark, all-encompassing *terror* which grips the character. The driving internal cause is revealed through *action* which then produces an effect.

Sound and Fury Signifying Nothing

The term 'effects' can sometimes be deadly, so easily luring actors into a contrived and false world. Take, for example, the following stage directions or 'effects' which George Bernard Shaw offers his actors in the play *Saint Joan*. These are all presented by Shaw as a reference to *how* the line is to be interpreted and then played. They are intended as *helpers* or *pointers* to playing the moment successfully:

- *interposing smoothly*
- *rising impetuously*
- *with a not too friendly smile*
- *playing the pink of courtesy*
- *furiously disappointed*
- *flushing angrily*
- *in a blaze of courage*
- *unabashed and rather roughly*

23

- with a mixture of cynical admiration and contempt
- distressed, but incapable of seeing the effect she is producing
- rising, with a flush of reckless happiness irradiating her face.

How easy it would be to simply embrace this end result and efficiently produce the desired theatrical effect. And how easy then for the audience's attention to be steadfastly fixed not upon the character's *situation*, but on the actor's *success* at achieving the form. The *effect* only draws attention to the form — the *cause* brings the audience towards true understanding and involvement.

Many playwrights and many, *many*, directors communicate their ideas and desires by describing the 'shell' which encases the effect they wish to create, i.e. look angrier, get sexier, be funnier *etc*. Actors must then decode or deconstruct the direction and find a justifiable and organic way of connecting to the *cause* which will *produce* the correct end result. Let's look more closely at another moment from *Saint Joan*. In Act One, Scene 2 Joan pleads her case to the Dauphin. She attempts to convince him to fight the English until they are banished from all of France and he is consecrated and crowned. He replies: 'I cannot do it. I am not built that way; and there is an end to it'. Shaw gives Joan's next line as: 'Blethers! We are all like that to begin with. I shall put courage into thee'.

The italics preceding her line read 'trenchant and masterful'. How are you then to say the line? Trenchantly and with great mastery, I suppose. Let's decode Shaw's instruction: 'Trenchant' can mean cutting, vigorous or scathing; 'masterful' can mean qualified or authoritative. Before we attach Joan's attitude to the exchange, let's look at her stimulus — the *cause*.

Charles' weak nature and pathetic inability to take responsibility make him totally dismissive of Joan's plea, replying: '... And there's an end to it'. Joan, however, vigorously denies his attitude through her action to *berate*: 'Blethers! We are all like that to begin with'. She then calls upon her defiant inner strength and knowledge and *empowers* him: 'I shall put courage into thee'. Her attitude when she berates him is self-assured, confident, full of *vigour*. And when she plays the action to empower, her steely and impassioned sense of right and absolute *authority* is harnessed.

Only then, through this inner process, will a trenchant and masterful manner be apparent and serve the play in the way Shaw intended.

You must always find the essential *essence* of any image or effect you need to inhabit — otherwise the image will not work. The 'angry' person may be found to be insecure; the 'hopeless' victim may be uncloaked to discover loneliness. The characters' actions need to spring from this integrated source, and through their *action*s we determine how others perceive them and the emotions which ensue.

Therefore, take your focus off *finding* a character and *creating* emotional states and commit firstly to what lies on the page: the facts, the action. Fulfil these requirements first and allow the rest to follow. This will lead to a connected and centred approach where you are open to the potential and the truth of the piece.

Don't Try, Allow

I was teaching a workshop at the University of California, San Diego a number of years ago. During the class we were doing a warm-up exercise called 'circle offers'. How this works is that in a circle of actors, one actor walks across the circle towards another. That actor says a line and makes some physical contact. The receiver doesn't respond verbally, but simply accepts the offer. He/she then moves across the circle to approach another actor with a *new* offer. This proceeds until all the actors have made and received various offers.

The focus of the exercise is on the actor as both receiver and transmitter; the two fundamental aspects of acting. These two dynamics must be honed and active in performance so the stage action can flow through each actor and create cause and effect. In other words, through our sensory reception we accept each stimulus; it makes its imprint upon our emotions and we therefore react, affecting someone else in turn. This process drives the play and directs its journey.

The 'circle offers' exercise allows each actor time to clearly *transmit* the offer in an effort to affect change within the listener. The *receiver* has time to simply accept the stimulus, without any concern to create a scene.

One actor in our workshop chose the line 'I love you'. He approached another actor and proceeded to 'act out' the moment, which he filled to the brim with emotion and with a strong sense of 'character'. The offer was, inevitably, swamped by emotion. The receiver wasn't affected because the actor had essentially had much more effect upon *himself*, because that was where his focus lay. He believed that if *he* could feel and experience the offer (the love), then it must be real. The only information we, as the audience, received through this moment was what *mood* the character was experiencing. In dramatic terms, this is an inactive choice as it doesn't produce *action* — it doesn't develop the dramatic situation. Onstage, every moment must be a movement into the *future* .

After asking him to repeat the offer more simply and to allow more *contact* — *trusting* the action through the physical gesture — the actor realised what was needed. But his search led him *further* within. He so desperately wanted to 'be' someone in an effort to produce 'the moment', the desired effect, that he began squeezing the text for meaning; he stammered the line; and his physical gestures towards the receiver were tense. After a dozen attempts, and with his frustration building, we tried something else.

I asked him to stand neutrally and to look clearly at the other actor's face — her eyes, lips — to see the offer within *her* rather than within *himself* — to allow his senses to *receive* the stimulus before him. Then, I asked him to simply commit to the physical gesture of touch: to allow this to guide him and to become his focus; to trust the *action*. Once this connection was made and he relinquished his mental grip on the form, his fingers became his release mechanism. Consequently, the sensory association triggered by this action led him and informed all he did. The line then flowed with such ease and clarity, affecting the receiver and creating a very intimate and powerful moment between them. The choice became *active*; the play moved forward.

The actor had discovered he didn't need to *supply* the scene with emotion, that the scene could create circumstances where the emotion became *unavoidable*. By accepting the other actor as the stimulus and then committing to the action, his *reaction* released him. Any sense of 'imitation' left him, and a pure, personal impulse was forged.

The Actor's Score

How do you go about uncovering the action? In life, as you know, we have a series of needs, moment by moment, which need fulfilling. We go about getting what we want through a series of physical *and* psychological actions. But often we are thwarted: obstacles emerge, either internally or externally, and we adjust our tactics and/or change objectives accordingly.

Stanislavsky called this our 'score' — as in a musical score. But, as opposed to *musical* notations which depict tempo, key, style and so on, our daily score depicts *thoughts, emotions* and *actions*. The character's score, which the actor must discover and plot during rehearsals, involves the same: a sequence of objectives revealed through physical and psychological expression.

Rehearsals are about uncovering the score of this expression, which will dynamically serve the actor's interpretation. This should enable the story you intend to tell being articulated via the play's *action*. Playwrights write plays and therefore words, not to be read, but *acted* — to be revealed through *action*. The script is merely the blueprint of this action. If you find the right action through discovering the *score*, the words simply flow.

> Conscious activity in preparing and rehearsing a role needed to be coherent and so organised as to create the conditions in which spontaneous, intuitive creation could occur... this is the sole purpose of *the system.*[9]

In the exercises that follow, we will study a number of speeches and reveal each scene's action to form our initial foundation. Once this important preparation work has been embraced the conditions are set for our next stage — creative exploration.

Chapter 4

Activating the Physical

Point of Concentration
In order to gain maximum benefit from your creative investigation, you need a secure point of focus for your energies.

The actor's 'point of concentration' offers three essential elements:
1. It focuses your energy.
2. It directs your concentration.
3. It gives you an aim to all you do on stage[10]

At an audition there are any number of points of concentration upon which you may focus before the approaching event. Two of the most popular are: 'I've *got* to get this job' and 'I'll *never* get this job'. As you will have no doubt experienced, concentrating on either of these can fuel self-consciousness and breed failure. However, you could trust in your preparation, and devote your entire energies to *'I want to present the emotional life of my character'*. This is the most positive, *practical,* and promising point of concentration.

How you go about *hosting* your own audition in this way requires thought and exploration. In the rehearsal of your piece your job is to pick the right point of concentration — the one which will activate and release you into the action — for each *moment* onstage. Once again, I am talking about the actor's *score*. Once plotted, the audition becomes about the *doing*, not the self-conscious *being.* In other words, you don't re-create the *form* in the hope of it being liked and accepted, but you re-inhabit the *structure* and lose yourself in the *doing.* As Stanislavsky said, if the body feels, the soul will respond. If you have mapped out the physical and psychological action of the scene, through committing to each of these moments, the emotional life will present itself and backup all you do and say. Many actors think they have to feel it before they can say it. However, you can also feel it *because* you say it. Trust that the words will lead you to the

29

experience for they are the residue of that experience.

What emerges from this approach? The full embodiment and release of the character's emotional life. And what were your auditioners hoping to witness during your all too brief time with them? Precisely that.

Your point of concentration is your springboard into the intuitive — it allows *perceiving* rather than *preconception* to occur. [12]

Once again, we are searching for approaches which will alleviate or indeed vanquish any sense of self-consciousness — the actor's major debilitator. Once you become overly aware of *how* what you are doing is being perceived, self-monitoring begins. You begin to judge your 'effects'. You cease to trust your organic and intuitive connections and an analytical and calculated mind-set takes over.

The camera which usually resides within, seeing what you see, suddenly becomes mobile. It tracks outside of you and then pans back, trapping you in its intense and critical glare. Under this harsh, unforgiving focus you seem to have little choice but to monitor and edit all you do and say, seeing yourself objectively and larger than life — a 70mm, Dolby sound play-back, running constantly and relentlessly through your head.

You continue acting however, remembering lines and moves, looking as competent as you can and working with your usual exterior efficiency and charm. But all the while an internal gladiatorial clash rages between two enemies — your creative connection versus your chief judge, censor and executioner. As an actor, you know who often wins.

Under these conditions, how can one expect to communicate effectively, reveal the authentic self and engage in any sort of fulfilling creative release?

One way I try to help actors when this occurs in an audition, is to reconnect them to their *physical lives*. Because our body-sense is so strong it only needs a small trigger to enable it to shed its imitation and re-engage its inner knowledge. It is sometimes suggested to actors that their speech be done in conjunction with a vital physical activity, such as playing racquet ball, squash, or shadow boxing. Often this physical focus relieves their speech of its vice-like pattern which the actor has imposed and a spontaneous 'aliveness' ensues. Often the sense becomes clearer, as the actor begins to *physically* inhabit the character's inner workings — receiving stimulus, processing its meaning, and then releasing a new energy based on the character's needs. When this begins to take place, self-consciousness departs, for it cannot be accommodated within these inner processes.

Obviously every speech cannot be staged by using a sport theme or intense activity, but the work we'll do shortly will be as vital, as physical, and as releasing. In these exercises we will choose specific points of concentration to help you to actualise your potential and discover the full experience your piece can offer.

After these intrinsic and organic connections have been forged, your camera will remain locked, unable to move. In your audition, when you feel stressed, under pressure and exposed, your full energy will flow freely into your creative invention.

As Lawrence Olivier said, the golden rule of acting is 'know exactly what you're going to do, *and then do it*'.

The Unknown Factor

One major cause of self-consciousness is that many actors, while performing their speech, try and second-guess what the auditioners are looking for. They voluntarily monitor each moment of their performance, adjusting any aspect of it if they sense this adjustment might be perceived as being more 'suitable'. So much energy expended on a false focus.

Ninety-nine times out of one hundred, you will *never* know what your auditioners are thinking or indeed what they want. *They* may not even know at this stage of their project. As soon as you walk in they may look at your height or hair colour and know casting you is, for whatever reason, impractical. To you, they now seem slightly disinterested, or worse still, *over-polite*. They offer you less time than the previous actor and tell you less about the project than you heard they would. This begins to rob you, second by painful second, of your belief in what you had prepared.

All you can do is act, according to what you know — based on the character/script/project — however inconclusive these facts may be. Then, with full empowerment, you must rest your point of concentration firmly on presenting the emotional life of the role as you see it, with the decisions as you have made them.

Of course you may be totally wrong in your interpretation. Given the scarcity of facts about the project and the absence of a complete script to read, you may have had to rely mostly on your imagination and sense of invention. If this is the case, then so be it.

Zan Sawyer-Daily, casting director for the Actor's Theatre of Louisville, told of an audition she witnessed where an actor came in to read for a new play. The audition scene sent out was one between a mother and her son. The actor's audition script however, only read 'WOMAN 1' and 'MAN 1'. Based on his feelings toward the scene, the actor concluded that the two characters were passionate lovers experiencing a tumultuous rift in their relationship. He arrived for his appointment, met all concerned with the project, and prepared to begin his audition. The *older* woman who had been hired to read opposite each person auditioning took her place on the set. The actor began his audition. He worked very well off the other actor: his choices all reflecting his belief about their turbulent relationship; his actions and gestures all informed by the dilemma in which he and his lover had found themselves. With a physical familiarity and assuredness, he touched, kissed and caressed his way through the scene, producing an acute intimacy between them and also revealing a deep emotional estrangement.

At the conclusion of the audition, the artistic director, casting director, producer, author and also the mature and very experienced other actor, sat looking toward the young actor, shocked and speechless. After some discussion, the mix-up eventually revealed itself. The actor had committed so completely to his interpretation, however, that he was offered the job — not only because of his obvious talent and preparedness, but also because his version of the scene had inspired the director to consider another dimension to the mother/son relationship previously unthought of.

This was, of course, a lucky coincidence, but the example still holds truth. What you present in your audition must be fully inhabited and fully crafted. It will then be clear that the package you present has been thoroughly worked through and conceived. If your *interpretation* was not what the auditioners were after, you'll have given them an opportunity to re-align your obvious talent into a different form. If *you* are not what they're after, they'll keep you in mind for the future. Why wouldn't they remember a solid, well-prepared, committed actor who cares about their work?

The House is Now Live

We have spoken of *your* point of concentration, but what are the *auditioner's* and *audience's* points of concentration? Before they focus on whether they like or dislike what they're viewing; if they feel it is appropriate or not; if they agree with the acting or it isn't what they were expecting; their *first* focus falls quite simply on, 'Do I *believe* this reality?'

And how will they perceive this reality or lack thereof? Through your *physical life*. Even if the *sound* of what you're doing seems real, their *visual* perception is where their belief firmly rests.

The Body Speaks

Everything your body says (and it won't lie) the audience will take in, digest, and make decisions upon. Therefore, you'd better be absolutely sure your body is registering exactly what you want the audience to receive. Tension, nerves, lack of preparation, running on adrenalin, hoping to 'please', wanting to 'impress' — these things will be physically manifest and take the auditioner's or audience's focus *off* the character and onto *you*.

To counteract this, be sure your rehearsal work *physically connects* you to the action, language, needs and images inherent in the piece, to your onstage environment and to those with whom you are interacting (imaginary or actual).

Reality can only be physical, in that it is received and transmitted through the sensory equipment. Through physical relationships all life onstage springs.[12]

In the rehearsal process we know that the intellect can inhibit and the emotions, being only states, are not the best points from which to begin your journey. Where then can you begin the exploration of your role? With what is most immediately available, with what responds most easily — your body.

An actor on the stage need only sense the smallest modicum of organic *physical* truth in his action or general state and instantly his emotions will respond to his inner faith and genuineness of what his body is doing. In our case it is incomparably easier to call forth real truth and faith within the region of our physical than of our spiritual nature. An actor need only believe in himself and his soul will open up to receive all the inner objectives and emotions of his role.[13]

The actor is a vessel into which another life pours — with different emotions, ideals and ways of dealing with the world. As actors you are conduits through which this new energy flows. You must allow these changes to affect you *physically,* for once your body feels, your soul will respond. As we discovered in Chapter Two, physical triggers activate emotional connections. To enable this to happen you must surrender to the circumstances around you and allow them to be the physical guide with which you start your journey into your new reality — the world of the play.

Improvising, whether verbal or non-verbal, can be a tremendous vehicle for this work, as it is a spontaneous, personal, instinctive response to a given stimulus or circumstance. It can personalise a situation or a moment for an actor instantaneously, at once fusing intellectual understanding with *sensation.*

Concepts are useless to actors unless they become *experiences.* Our minds can be cold, rational, logical and analytical. By intellectualising the experience, we can deaden our senses. The more we engage *physically*, the more our senses become alert and enlivened, therefore creating the possibility for powerful experiences. If our minds decrease the potency of the work, our bodies must become the antidote.

The exercises in this book have been designed for this specific purpose: to enable you to inhabit and be transformed by the dynamics of your scene. This will then forge a close relationship between all you do, say and feel, enabling this essential belief to be palpable for yourself and, of course, your audience.

Chapter 5

An Empty Stage at the Service of Invention [14]

Your exploration work on your chosen piece can and should be exciting. Getting a piece together for an audition presents a chance to work your craft and the actual audition presents the opportunity to *perform*. Embrace these opportunities as a part of your ongoing process as an actor. Every screen test, audition *and* interview presents moments where you 'do' your art. Seize them and enjoy!

Different processes and exercises trigger different responses in actors. The exercises in PART TWO of this book present an array of possibilities. But before we move on to the exercises, I would like to explain where my particular approach stems from. The class illustrated below consists of a series of exercises designed principally for scene work. These will give you a good indication of the potential of this approach when it comes to your solo monologue and will help to propel you imaginatively into the world of your scene.

Many of the exercises contained in this book were developed during a block of scene work I was teaching at The National Institute of Dramatic Art (NIDA) in Sydney during 1988. We had already had much input into the left side of our brains where data and information storage is processed and retained. This is always necessary during certain stages of training. But I felt it important at this time, and with this group of actors, to activate the right side of their brains where intuition, instinct and fantasy reside.

The Journey — Fact-finding

Firstly, after choosing their scenes and partners, the actors read the scenes to the class for *sense*. This was to be the foundation of all that would follow: Not how do I *feel* about what I'm saying, but what do I want to make *understood* as a *result* of what I am saying.

Finding the sense and establishing the meaning are two very distinct stages of this preliminary work. Discovering the *meaning* requires an emotional attachment which springs from the character's specific inner monologue and point of view at that instant. It also comes from the *physical sensations* which occur during the exchange. These you can discover on the rehearsal room floor. It is too soon at this stage to start supplying emotions and attaching them to the text. Spend time searching for the *sense* — the linear knowledge of *what* is being said, rather than *how* it is being said. Own and inhabit the thoughts which the character is communicating. In other words, avoid final solutions and penetrate the character's thinking process.

This naturally led us into discussing the action, that is, what happens in the scene, what events take place. We then asked how these events are affected by the context of the play: i.e. What do they offer the play? How do they move the play and its themes forward? What would the play lose if the scene was to be cut?

This is an excellent way of pinpointing function. The actor's fundamental question should be: 'How does this scene contribute to the reason why the play was written?' Indeed, how does every *moment* of my performance contribute? Robert Benedetti often speaks of this as a sure fire way for the actor to be able to identify why the scene is integral to the play and what responsibilities the actor has in facilitating the telling of the story.

We then looked at the general *beats* within the scene (see EXERCISE 2). That is, when the focus of the scene changed radically, or when a character's wants altered sufficiently for the scene to change course as a result. We noted any *atmospheric* changes — where temperature or any other outside stimulus affected the mood of the scene. This ultimately helped to reveal the main events and any crisis which led to an event.

That was our preparation stage. It allowed us to acknowledge *what* was on the page in terms of language, plot, action and the playwright's structure. *How* we were to perform it and *why* the characters said what they did, were not discussed. But through this work the actors became very familiar with the lines (as the scenes were quite short), which enabled us to move easily to the next stage of the process.

A Secure World
Each pair then built a *four-walled environment* in which their scene could exist, for example, the lounge, the caravan, the boardroom. It was four-walled because I wanted the actor's focus to be entirely on

their scene partner and the interaction within their environment. I wanted to take away the need to 'present' or 'perform' the scene and 'play it out front'. It was to be an intimate and private exchange between the characters without them thinking at all of the audience. This was a rehearsal, not a performance, and the experience for the actor was to be one of *being*, not *proving*.

The centre of the rehearsal room was claimed as a 'timeless' and 'placeless' region — a 'twilight zone' where the raw dynamics, truths and issues of the scene, could be explored and battled out free from naturalism, circumstantial restraints and appropriateness. It was a blank canvas where the characters' inner worlds, emotional lives and potentials could be experienced and released to the full.

The actors were free at any time to depart to this arena, to instinctively follow an impulse, to discover a depth or quality within the scene and to pursue it, then take it back onto their 'set' and allow it to affect and inform the scene and its atmosphere.

Extending the Boundaries

Some of the 'departures' offered to the actors to explore in this twilight zone were:

• Without words, transform the scene's journey into *heightened movement,* culminating in the main event of the scene at the end of one minute.

• Sum up your character's major 'want' *in one word.* Using this word and that of your partner's, improvise and battle the two issues against one another. That is, control *vs* independence, power *vs* respect, indulgence *vs* abstinence, revenge *vs* honour.

• Sit back-to-back with your partner and begin the scene, simply contacting each of the ideas. After each line, take turns with your partner to say, *'And again'*. The line is then repeated until the *idea* behind it is revealed clearly. You may say *'And again'* three of four times per line.

• Lie on the ground facing your partner. Cover your scripts with one hand. Then uncover your scripts line by line and communicate each thought to each other through *eye contact* only. Observe major punctuation, i.e. **?** . **!**

• Experience the journey of the scene using only *one word* from each line. Choose a word which carries the essence of the line.

• Take any beat from the scene and *explore and heighten*: the love; the humour; the conflict; the discoveries (see EXERCISE 3).

- Stand back-to-back and say each line accompanied by a *heightened physical action* which sums up the idea or thought behind it.
- Do the scene, prefacing each line with *'And then he/she decides to say...'*. This clarifies the character's choice and reminds you to enter their moment-by-moment thought process.
- Do the scene, making *physical contact* on every line, no matter how fleeting. Repeat this, avoiding touching the arms of the other person. Repeat again, this time avoiding using your hands as the means of contact.
- As you move around the space, explore without the use of speech the *physical relationship* and *dynamics of the characters' interaction.* For example, who is the hunter and who the prey? Who is the visionary and who the follower? Who holds the status and power physically, emotionally? When does it change? How? What does each character stand to gain or lose from the other?
- Choose *four issues* the character is fighting for. For example, love, honour, repentance, deception, forgiveness, betrayal. Improvise using your four words and those of your partner. Allow the issues to clash as you pursue your needs.
- Do the scene *without words*, exploring the journey of the scene, beat by beat, through eye contact only.
- Move around the space. *Freeze* every five seconds, exploring some aspect of your relationship to the other character. Use distance, closeness, levels and heights and gestures. Fill the space, ensuring that throughout the exercise you reveal the variety of needs alive and at work within the relationship.
- *Swap characters* in the scene.
- Without words, *contact the environment,* the surrounding *atmosphere* and your partner's *presence.* Experience this atmosphere in which the scene resides and springs from, without drama or acting. Feel the air around you become charged.
- After you say your line, *mumble your inner monologue* aloud under your partner's line. This should propel and fuel your next line and exchange (see EXERCISE 4).
- After each of your partner's lines, ask out loud, *'Is this good or bad for me?'* Then quickly process his or her offer, decide how you feel, and allow that information to inform your next choice and subsequent line (see EXERCISE 5).
- After exploring the scene's journey through heightened movement, choose *three physically repeatable motifs* which sum up or

embrace your character's needs. One must involve your legs, one your arms, and one your torso. Improvise with your partner using these motifs.

• Repeat the exercise above, now using both *your* three movements *and* those of your partner. You may use his or her motifs to question them or taunt them.

• After each line, *mumble your need*. For example: 'Come here now.' (*I can't bear to be alone!*) 'Why should I believe you?' (*He's losing ground — pursue him)* (see EXERCISE 7).

• Whilst moving, and in your own time, explore your character's *personal space-* the space around them which they deem to be their property, it may be three inches or twelve feet. Define this space, then *double* it. Find the degree of space most appropriate for your character. Now decide how the character *affects this air* around him or her as he or she moves: Is the air heavy and pushed? Light and floating? Erratic, dangerous, sharp? *Double* its dynamic, explore the sensations, then allow it to become more subtle. But first, push the boundaries.

• Decide on the character's energy centre: is it the head, the heart or gut, where the energy is mostly centred? Double its speed and force. Be driven and consumed by this motor. Allow these dynamic changes to inform the character's inner life so to heighten the experience of 'living' your character.

• Along with your partner, choose a line each from the scene and *explore your relationship* through that line whilst moving around the space. Explore the exchange through speed, the distance between you, levels and heights.

• Whilst moving around the space, accentuate the characters' *public persona* or image presented to the other. Claim it, embody it, exaggerate it. Then, release its *private* self — the one they shield from the other. Embody it, explore its energy and hidden needs. With your partner, snap in and out of these two worlds and inhabit both sets of dynamics. Experience any tension between the two.

• Whilst walking around, contemplate the character's *ultimate fantasy ending* to the scene. Regardless of whether it happens or not, or *could* ever happen, choose the ultimate climax to the scene. Run to a private part of the room, and spend ten seconds by yourself living this ending. *Experience* the murder, the sacrifice, the love, the redemption, the betrayal or the ecstasy.

• Stand six metres from your partner. See a part of their character you want to touch — a part you love, cherish, respect, are turned-on by. Take thirty seconds to walk towards your partner, preparing to touch and embrace that part. Stop at twenty-nine seconds and a few centimetres from an actual touch. Allow this quality of your partner's to 'imprint' upon your entire body during your journey towards him or her.

• Repeat the exercise as above, but choose a part of your partner's character you despise or resent, a part you'd like to tear or smash or by which you are frightened. Take thirty seconds for the journey. Prepare your fist, feel the knife. Spend the last ten seconds preparing to follow through with your desired action in slow-motion. Stop at twenty-nine seconds and a breath away from the action.

• Walk around the space, keeping eye contact with your partner. See both of the qualities chosen above within him or her. Experience these *opposite dynamics* and allow them to affect the way you move through space and your non-verbal interchange.

And so the departures continued. All aimed to balance the work we had already done, with the *adventure* the scene has to offer. Some of the scenes I have worked on using the above approach have included May and Eddie from Shepard's *Fool For Love*, Francis and Betsheb from Nowra's *The Golden Age*, Trigorin and Arardina from Chekhov's *The Seagull*, Tom and Meg from Gow's *Away* and Barbara and Douglas in Gow's *Europe*, Platonov and Anna Petrovna from Chekhov's *Wild Honey*, Peter and Jerry from Albee's *Zoo Story*, and Leontes and Hermione from Shakespeare's *The Winter's Tale*.

It was quite amazing to witness the discoveries that were made in the free-wheeling, reckless 'zone' in the middle of the room, and to see how these discoveries ignited the interchange on the actor's return to their set. The scene became layered and took on a bold physicality, opposites were found, the actors embodied the language and released their energies with ease. The inner monologues became potent and fuelled the action. The actors began to want their partners not to *feel* what they were feeling, but to *understand* what they were saying. This is so very often a trap in acting — the need to emote. Lisle Jones often says, 'Acting is not about doing what you feel, but feeling what you have to do'.

Because of this clarity of thought the story became clear, the action defined, the choices and decisions sharp and specific. As a result the 'blocking' or physical life of the scene also took care of itself. If I was directing the scene I would now be in a position to work *reactively* from what was happening on the floor, as opposed to actively suggesting, motivating or 'moving' the scene because the actors were waiting to be told what to do.

This type of work can lend itself more appropriately to certain plays or scenes. Obviously the more physical and emotionally 'muscular', the better. But all drama needs to be extreme and profound no matter how subtly it may demand to be played, or how small the aperture through which you express it. For ultimately, subtlety is just a tightening of the focus in order to intensify.

These exercises are triggers to stimulate the most athletic responses to the character's interior landscape. Once experienced *physically*, they now reside within the character's range; they have been recorded on the character's tape or disk. How you wish to embody and *express* your character's needs now rests in your chosen interpretation and the terrain you wish to cover, given the vision of the production.

I have adapted the above work to aid your *solo* preparation and rehearsal of your audition speech. The exercises in PART TWO provide you with more specific ways to do this.

Damage Control

Sadly, the type of powerful and organic exploration outlined above, which is often the foundation work of many ensembles, is viewed cynically by many actors. They are either wary of its content and dubious of its results, or find the entire approach simply implausible.

Interestingly though, when these actors speak of their most remarkable audience experience to date, they mostly name the world's great ensembles. And what would be their fantasy future career? To be a part of a company whose work is based on the ensemble experience.

Why do actors seek this experience and imagine the opportunity will offer great nourishment? What creative sustenance will be digested to revitalise their souls? Why do they intuitively believe that vastly new and perhaps uncharted dimensions to their work will be ignited? The great luxury of 'time' is one reason. We often hear that a particular production was twelve months in the making and bemoan the fact we have but five weeks. We should note that often within that twelve-month period perhaps up to *five* different plays were being rehearsed. What else lies beneath our longing? For many, the ensemble embodies the artistic trilogy: the team, the trust, the process.

The Team, the Trust, the Process

These three magical elements combine to create an environment with *permission to play* at its core. The rehearsal *process* takes place in a creative arena where the *physical, organic,* inner connections to the world of the play and its characters are forged. Through a philosophical union of beliefs, the *team* affirms the journey ahead and produces a collective courage in all you undertake.

Then there's the other essential ingredient — the *trust.* I've often observed great productions and searched for how this ever-present trust manifests itself onstage. I believe it resides in the *rapport* between the players. A powerful and immediate *intimacy* underpins each moment. To my mind, this promotes a sensory and even *sensual* relationship between the play, the players and the audience. This unique energy creates a special experience and leads to that stage 'aura' we sometimes label atmosphere.

> Each performance should have an atmosphere which does not belong to anyone but belongs to the performance itself... the heartbeat... atmosphere gives us the air, the space around us. It coaxes our deeper feelings and emotions, our dreams... Without atmosphere we are imprisoned on the stage.[15]

With the team, trust and process, we, as actors, believe we at last can leave the world of imitation and uncover our unique creative voice. Due to time restraints, inadequate direction and insubstantial material, we are often forced into fabricating our acting in order to survive in our industry. Sadly, the audience has not only learnt to accept this fabrication but to *expect* it. As actors we believe the ensemble experience will release us and re-dress this lethal habit.

The Actor's Centre

One of the main reasons for my desire to establish The Actors' Centre in Sydney in 1987 was to offer an environment where true experimentation could take place — where, free from commercial pressures, actors could extend and expand their craft, re-evaluate and reinforce their skills and take those risks so essential to their continued creative development (*see* Plates 3 & 8). Now seven years old, we still search for new ways in which the Centre can be of benefit and how it may attract more members of the profession.

Fear holds many back from creative risk-taking. Fear of what? Are we scared of getting it wrong? What is 'it' anyway? What is this mythical 'correctness', hanging like a noose around our necks, strangling our creative courage and thwarting our sense of self?

In the Theatre De Complicité's production of *The Winter's Tale*, the company's director Simon McBurney was performing the role of Leontes. One of the most extraordinary scenes came in Act 3 when we discover that, because of his belief in Hermione's death, Leontes has chosen as his penance to crawl daily to the grave of his wife. In most productions this is accepted as a metaphorical statement. But here, it was *fact*. To see Leontes' bound and bloodied knees driving relentlessly into the earth, with the entire company also on their knees suffering the shame and bitterness by which he is consumed, was an immensely compelling theatrical statement.

Where did this choice come from? We can only imagine the actor gave himself the license to fall to the rehearsal room floor, remain there, and experiment with this potent physical impulse to see where it may lead. One second of self-doubt — 'Perhaps it won't work... What am I doing anyway? I might look stupid' — and the choice may never have found its way into the show's powerful landscape.

Indeed, without the entire company not only acknowledging but supporting his bold choice it may *not* have worked. But you will never know the extent of your creative ingenuity if you are not prepared to risk, then validate afterwards. If the idea doesn't work, drop it; if it serves your purpose, keep it, craft it, incorporate it.

Creative Independence

At the Academy, Lisle Jones often reminds the actors not to mistake 'the wish for the deed'. As a young actor in training I too used to wish with every fibre of my brain that I could make it work — somehow get it right. And I believed that if I was very, very lucky, and things perhaps fell into place, I might pull through and be cloaked in a reality deemed creative and believable. But my brain, the cold analytical computer, ruled my search, creating effort and contaminating almost every stage of the journey. In the rehearsal room, I was at the mercy of every silent opinion surrounding me. The worst, of course, being the toughest and most ruthless critic residing within. I was beginning to discover that if you don't act what you're compelled to act, then you act nothing.

But by changing my point of concentration from my actor's *fear* to the character's *beliefs*, effectively moving from my brain as the source of my motivation to my heart, 'deeds' began to replace the fruitless 'wishes' and I was able to unplug from my lethal mind-set based on luck, chance and fate. Rehearsals became a time of release, an *expedition* as opposed to a test of talent and validity. I had at last surrendered to the creative process, by allowing myself the permission, finally, to play.

In Sanskrit, the root of the verb 'to be' is 'to grow'.

The Next Step

So once again you need to remind yourself, 'I am scared, *and...*'. To help you to fully actualise your potential through your audition work, I offer the following opportunities. Hopefully through your experience of them you may even be able to say, 'I am *powerful, and...*'.

Each exercise is fully explained, its application described, your point of concentration outlined and various illustrations offered. They provide many exciting challenges and I'm sure they will prove stimulating for your work *beyond* the audition as well. The arena for creative risk-taking can extend from the audition to the rehearsal to the studio, and can include anyone who is also willing to break the boundaries of his or her creative expression. Commit to the adventure ahead. Best of luck!

PLATE 1
'Now't more outcastin...' Lisa Baumwol as Ayre in Louis Nowra's *The Golden Age*, directed by Dean Carey.

PLATE 2
'But all is not lost, oh no!' A scene from Ivan Turgenev's *A Month in the Country*, with Roxane Wilson as Natalia Petrovna. Directed by Dean Carey.

PLATE 3
Heidi Lapaine in the Actor's Centre presentation of *Lulu* by Franz Wedekind.

PLATE 4
'The ambition in my love thus plagues itself...' Jennifer Botica rehearses
Helena from *All's Well That Ends Well*.

PLATE 5

'But now he's gone, and my idolatrous fancy must sanctify his relics.'
Again, Jennifer Botica rehearses Helena from *All's Well That Ends Well*.

PLATE 6
'I once told you, Marianne, you wouldn't escape my love...' John Adam
and Deborah Galands in the final scene from Odon Von Horvath's *Tales
From the Vienna Woods*. Directed by Dean Carey.

PART TWO

The Creative Arena

Rehearsal Room Exercises

EXERCISE 1: Extend/Advance

This exercise originated from Keith Johnstone's work at The Loose Moose Theatre Company in Calgary. It was designed to allow improvisers a way of enhancing any offers which emerged in a scene. An 'offer' can be an idea, a reaction, a suggestion, a decision — any major stimulus that affects the scene and the players.

Explanation Firstly, the exercise enabled the performers to acknowledge the offer which was to be focused upon, then it gave them time to extend and amplify the offer, which advanced the scene, in turn developing the action.

The idea was that after the offer had been explored in this way the energy created around the offer would be of sufficient 'charge' and detail that it was now unavoidable to those in the scene. They would then begin to work *re-actively* off the offers which surrounded them. This enabled them to take the focus off pushing and straining to make the scene 'happen', and to simply embrace the possibilities as they presented themselves.

Application Using this basic concept, I have adapted its use to the audition speech. This exercise offers the actor an opportunity to plunge into each of the ideas and to physically and emotionally explore exactly what lies behind or indeed beyond the words. As I have mentioned before, it fuses at once intellectual understanding with *sensation* and aims to pinpoint the precise energy fuelling each thought.

Point of concentration To verbally unearth the dominant meaning beyond the words.

ILLUSTRATION 1
Extend/Advance can be done with someone else side-coaching or you can select the moments yourself.

Clear a space so you have some room to move. You may need to

46

have your script open and accessible as once you begin extending you may lose your place in the text.

Take a moment to focus your energies on the scene. Allow yourself to imaginatively connect to the person you are interacting with or, if the character is alone, to the situation or dilemma facing him or her.

When you're ready, say the first line. Then choose *one word* or an *image* in the line that you wish to explore. Say the word, then extend its meaning using your own words and phrases. For example, if the word is 'large', you could extend by saying: 'large... big... enormous... gigantic... powerful... awesome... *overwhelming*'.

Note: Be sure you extend based on *sensation*. In other words, avoid extending in a monotone as if you were reading from a Thesaurus. It's not mental and verbal gymnastics. Let your *sensory impulses* enter the exercise. Only then will you uncover the essence of each thought and connect emotionally.

'Large' can mean all of the definitions listed above and more. But 'overwhelming' may be exactly the thought which lies behind the word. As you extend, this detailing allows you time to live with the thought, to ruminate on its meaning. If the line was, 'This is a very large problem for me', by allowing the thought *'overwhelming'* to affect the word 'large', it changes the choice and specifies what you are trying to make understood with the idea. Now try saying the line aloud with this thought in mind and feel how easy it is to inhabit the line now that the idea behind it has been uncovered. Communication becomes active and you will feel your energy releasing.

Michael Shurtleff states that 'communication is duplication'; you're attempting to duplicate your thoughts and feelings within the other character, to gain the desired reaction or response. Many actors get too locked into their character's overall objective. This objective is *not* the major focus of the scene- the main priority is to change the other person's *will*. You have more chance of achieving this if you cease worrying about making them *feel* what you're feeling and allow them to *understand* your feelings, moment by moment. Only through uncovering the specific idea behind each thought will you achieve accurate and effective communication.

You may find through working with this exercise that your choice of 'overwhelming' makes the character too much of a victim and is not appropriate for that point in the play. Therefore, extend again in another direction, such as 'large... difficult... tricky... elusive... provocative... *challenging!*

Now the choice has shifted. The character has changed his or her attitude toward the situation and the idea behind the thought has altered. We receive different information from the character through his or her exchange. By exploring the possibilities of what may work best for the scene, you clarify each choice and its meaning, and in turn create the *score*.

Of course, working in this detail produces the other essential component of your speech — ownership. Through using *Extend/ Advance* you will *personalise* each thought, *claim* its essential energy, and it will become (if done correctly) *sensation*.

This will then form part of the physical infrastructure of your piece. In your rehearsal you will have inhabited the *physical dynamics* associated with the words. If done in enough detail, these dynamics will be triggered again by the sheer act of *saying* the words in the audition.

The effect is much like when you look back through an old photograph album. Because you have experienced (personalised) all of the sensations associated with each and every photo, you don't have to work to produce sensation. The image triggers all the required sets of responses. You simply allow each stimulus entry, and your reactions take care of themselves. The emotional landscape or backdrop to each 'offer' has already been prepared. The same vivid associations occur with particular songs we hear which plug into a certain experience or time in our lives.

Trust then in your rehearsal preparation and at your audition (much like the photograph album) simply focus on each offer line by line, and react to them as they present themselves.

Note: After using this exercise on text you may find each thought becomes overloaded with meaning. By immersing yourself in that meaning the line may appear overly emphasised. The next stage is to trust the work you have done and allow it to affect your acting in whatever way you feel is most appropriate to the character and the situation.

ILLUSTRATION 2

Using *Extend/Advance*, let's look in detail at Natalia Petrovna's scene from Ivan Turgenev's, *A Month in the Country*. Natalia has, unknowingly, fallen in love with her ward's tutor. Vera, after extensive and provocative questions from Natalia, finally declares *her* love for the young, handsome Beliaev. Upon hearing the child's innocent admission, Natalia suddenly feels faint and distressed and sends Vera from the room. She attempts to deal with her strange and disconcerting emotional dilemma. Let's look at her first four lines:

NATALIA: *These children love each other... Well, it's a touching idea, and may Heaven bless them both. The way she came out with it... and I with no idea* — (laughing feverishly) — *ha!* (Rising, vehement.) *But all is not lost — oh no...'*

We'll now apply *Extend/Advance* to unearth what may be driving each thought:

'*These children love each other...*' Extend '*children*' — children... innocents... vulnerable beings... *young pure lovers*. Advance: '*Well, it's a touching idea...*'. Extend '*touching*' — touching... simple... pleasant... *quaint*. Advance: '*... And may Heaven bless them both*'. Extend '*bless*' — bless... anoint... keep safe... look after... *guard and protect*. Advance: '*The way she came out with it...* '. Extend '*out with it*' — out with it... blurting it forth... freely expressing... captivating in its innocence... *an absolute admission*. Advance: '*and I with no idea*'. Extend '*no idea*' — no idea... not the faintest clue... never suspected... never dreamed of... *couldn't have possibly expected*. Advance: '*ha!*'. Extend '*ha!*' — ha!... quite extraordinary!... I never expected this!... An absolute surprise!... *Quite a substantial shock!!!* Advance: '*But all is not lost, oh no...*'. Extend '*not lost*' — not lost... not forsaken... within my grasp... *still ultimately achievable!*

Through the extensions Natalia's interior world becomes more defined. She's taken aback by Vera's honesty and vulnerability *(young pure lovers)*, and her efforts to shield and detach herself from the hurt and her inevitable downfall become clear *(It's a touching idea.)*. You have now begun to process the thoughts, forming personal responses to each idea. Her attitude to her situation has become defined (see Plate 2).

The journey through your extensions can lead you from your *head*, as a place where the thoughts originate, to your *heart*, where you feel certain emotions and sensations, to your *centre* — the pit of your stomach where instinct and 'gut' reactions reside. It's this third level where raw and highly concentrated connections are forged.

To assist actors in remembering these connections, I ask them to repeat the line after the extension. For example, with the extension on the word 'touching', we hit upon the word 'quaint'. Retaining this attitude of slight condescension and jealousy, repeat the entire line, 'Well, it's a *touching* idea...'. This allows the discoveries made during the extension to inform the line when repeated. There's not much point embarking on a tremendously potent exploration of the thought's essence if on your return the line retains its original attachments and quality.

The same applies to the next extension: 'bless'. After uncovering *'guard and protect'*, retain her attitude of mock care and seeming unperturbed resignation and repeat the line with both extensions: 'Well, it's a *touching* idea, and may Heaven *bless* them both.'

ILLUSTRATION 3

You may also want to extend *within* an extension. For example, during the last extension on 'not lost', we arrived at *'still ultimately achievable'*. This uncovered Natalia's selfishness and her ability for deceitful manipulation. Allowing this to fuel your journey, extend *'achievable'* — achievable... capable of being embraced... winnable... *I refuse to lose*. Extend *'lose'* — lose... be lost... forgotten... thrown on the heap... discarded... *grow old*. Extend *'grow old'* — grow old... become aged... withered... decrepit and despised... never having *tasted passion*. Extend *'tasted'* — touched... stroked... caressed... *entwined*. Extend *'passion'* — passion... romance... unbridled sensuality... ultimate sacrifice... complete union... *pleasure beyond all limits!!*

Now, allow the depth of this journey to rocket you back to the beginning of the line, keeping all that you have found: *'But all is not lost — oh no...'*. The full scope of Natalia's fear and power begins to emerge.

This work enlivens the unconscious, provoking deep associations and strong energy productions — your speech is charged with your imprint and your acting is informed.

The example from *A Month in the Country* shows *Extend/Advance* working on a soliloquy. It can prove as effective in a slightly different way when dealing with a scene. On these extensions, not only can you explore the *images* but also the *effect* you wish to have on the other character. In other words, if when you're extending you find you begin to challenge, confront, cajole, entreat, then allow the extension to amplify *this*. As such, both your *connection* to the thought *and* the way you *communicate* that thought become more specific.

ILLUSTRATION 4

Take a scene in Arthur Miller's *All My Sons*. George returns to the Keller household to stop his sister, Ann, from marrying the son of Joe Keller, whom George believes is responsible for his father's imprisonment.

> GEORGE: *Annie, we did a terrible thing. We can never be forgiven. Not even to send him a card at Christmas.*

Using these first few lines we'll extend both the image and the effect being created.

'*Annie, we did a terrible thing.*' Extend '*terrible*' — terrible... cruel... we punished our father wrongly... you and I abused him and caused him great pain... it was *wrong and we were fools*.

The effect on Ann could be one of *admonishment*.

Advance: '*We can never be forgiven*'. Extend '*never*' — never... as long as we live... no matter how hard we try or how much we beg to be unburdened of the guilt... we are *forever tainted*.

The effect here may be one of *illumination*.

Advance: '*Not even to send him a card at Christmas*'. Extend '*not even*' — not even... we couldn't even muster that... not even an attempt or a gesture... we were so full of self-righteousness... so sure of ourselves.... absolutely *high and mighty* .

George now *ridicules* himself and Ann in an effort to make her understand the consequences of their actions.

Extend/Advance helps gain specific and detailed connections to the inner life of the character and allows your *score* to be revealed and clarified. Use it whenever you feel a deeper contact and a greater degree of specificity is needed.

EXERCISE 2: Speeches Within Speeches

Choosing Your Beats
Let us now look at beats and how a speech can be divided into certain units of action. Once you have chosen your beats you can then explore and heighten certain aspects of them in order to test their dynamic potential.

Explanation Each beat (sometimes called a unit) revolves around or concerns itself with, an issue — an aspect of the character's situation or dilemma. A beat is a section of the text or a group of thoughts which deal with this specific part of the character's objective.

Much like you acknowledge the punctuation in the speech to help claim the thought process, plotting the beats is like deciphering the scene's *psychological* punctuation. If the structure of each sentence is a direct expression of the character's thought process, the structure of the beats is a direct expression of the character's emotional process.

Robert Benedetti points out that the stylistics of language reflect the personality and characteristics of the speaker, and to enter the character's consciousness you must claim not only what the character says, but *how* he or she says it. This applies also to the psychological journey — claim not only what happens to the character, but also the sequence and consequence of *how* it affects him or her. The beats represent and clarify this journey. The actor can then feel no longer burdened with the weight of attempting to achieve the scene's full depth and power through every moment. But he or she can trust the *journey* which has been securely plotted, and allow the *sum* of all the individual moments and beats to produce the scene's impact.

Once the beats have been uncovered you may want to assign each of them a name or title (see Plate 2). This is *not* done as an intellectual exercise but as a way of plotting the emotional journey through the scene. It will help you to avoid the speech becoming one entire entity embellished with one emotion or set of responses. Lisle Jones always suggests the actor 'find the speeches *within* the speech'.

Application To avoid scenes and indeed speeches from being swamped by a particular dynamic and emotional bias. By plotting the beats, we aim to uncover the *structure* of the speech. This structure becomes a pathway along which we can plot the character's journey. From here, we ensure maximum emotional range and specific detail.

Point of concentration Through our experience of the speech, we aim to locate major shifts in the scene's energy and direction.

ILLUSTRATION 1

Let's look at a scene from *Wild Honey* by Anton Chekhov, translated and adapted by Michael Frayn. Following is one version of the speech divided into *five* beats. It often comes down to your own interpretation and no one way is the correct way.

Anna Petrovna has followed her potential lover Platanov into the garden at night. Both of them, married to other partners (she now widowed), bemoan the fact that their lives have gone in separate directions. Their discussion leads to an unspecified past 'liaison' which Platanov seemingly dismisses as a figment of her imagination. Turning towards him, the forest surrounding them and a midsummer night's breeze touching the air, she responds:

ANNA PETROVNA: *How can you say that? How can you lie to me, on such a night as this, beneath such a sky? Tell your lies in the* ①
autumn, if you must, in the gloom and the mud, but not now, not here. You're being watched! Look up, you absurd man! A thousand eyes, all shining with indignation! You must be good and true, just ②
as all this is good and true. Don't break this silence with your little words! ...

There's no man in the world I could ever love as I love you.
There's no woman in the world you could ever love as you love me.
Let's take that love; and all the rest, that so torments you — we'll ③
leave that to others to worry about.

Such a solemn face! It's a woman who's come to call, not a wild animal! All right — if you really hate it all so much I'll go away again. Is that what you want? I'll go away, and everything will be just as it was before. Yes...?
(She laughs.)
Idiot! Take it! Snatch it! Seize it! What more do you want? Smoke ④
it to the end, like a cigarette — pinch it out — tread it under your heel. Be human!
(She gently shakes him.)
You funny creature! A woman who loves you — a woman you love — fine summer weather. What could be simpler than that?...

You don't realise how hard life is for me. And yet life is what I long
for. Everything is alive nothing is ever still. We're surrounded by ⑤
life. We must live, too, Misha! Leave all the problems for tomorrow.
Tonight, on this night of nights, we'll simply live!

A fairly convincing argument! As you can see, I have marked *five*
beats. Each beat can be viewed as a separate speech within the
speech. This will assist us in opening up the scene's range to produce
a dynamic emotional journey.

Now, look at each beat in detail — observe the major thrust of that
beat. What similar ideas fuel the beat ? Which of the character's
needs drives it, and what does the character wish to achieve ? If there
was one *key phrase* which summed up that beat or unit, which would
it be? For example:

Beat 1: No lies... *'not now, not here'*.
Beat 2: *'Don't break this silence...'*
Beat 3: *'Let's take that love...'*
Beat 4: *'Be human!'*
Beat 5: *'...we'll simply live!'*

These lines distil the character's specific wants, beat by beat. They
also clearly show the speech's journey. It is much like an exercise
where you concentrate your scene down to a telegram format, which
demands you choose the half dozen most important moments without
which the speech would not make sense. It enables you to narrow the
aperture to focus on the speech's essence, so the major turning points
and events become palpable.

Remember: working for form and end results can significantly
reduce range and ownership. Many actors have worked this piece
with me, *beginning* their rehearsal process by attempting to inhabit
Anna Petrovna's feisty nature, her sensuality, passion and
independence. Yes, she is all these things, but they are by-products of
the *action* of the scene — what *happens*. *This* must be our starting
point.

Therefore the journey for Anna Petrovna begins with Beat 1 — her
refusal to accept Platanov's way of looking at their relationship (don't
lie... *'not now, not here'*). In Beat 2 she requests he doesn't say
anything to contaminate the intimacy possible between them *('Don't
break this silence with your little words')*. In Beat 3 she proposes she

54

and Platanov, against all the odds, rejuvenate their passion and commitment *('Let's take that love...')*. In Beat 4, because of Platanov's hopeless outlook he resists his feelings and instincts, provoking her to exclaim: *'Be human!'*. He now begins to be affected by her vulnerability, and so in Beat 5 she expounds one final thought, made of reckless passion and graceful ease: *'Tonight, on this night of nights, we'll simply live!'*

Actors so often view the speech as a total entity and find one or two dynamics or qualities which, as mentioned earlier, can swamp the entire text. Each of the five sections can now be explored for their *unique* and *essential* energy, enabling you to extend the character's and the scene's range. EXERCISE 3 will begin this work but let's first look more closely at Beats.

Beat Changes

Explanation The next thing to explore is what initiates one beat to end and another to begin. Something must *happen* for the scene to change direction. These moments are called *beat changes*, and denote an *event*. Beat changes occur when a character changes objective, or alters his or her tactics sufficiently to create a new energy in the scene, *or* achieves his or her desired result and a new objective begins. Sometimes they can be spotted clearly on the page but other times they will emerge only through the playing of the scene and through your *experiencing* of the action.

Application When you have plotted the beat changes it means by necessity you have observed the events through the speech. Plays are written about events: crises, disclosures, deceits, tragedies, triumphs, reconciliations — occurrences which speak of the human condition.

Playwrights register and record the tremors of this world.[16]

These 'tremors' manifest themselves in the events which the characters experience. Once acknowledged through your acting, they begin to release the play's action. The nature and impact of these events will then chart an emotional journey which, to our best knowledge, will articulate the playwright's intentions.

How you plot beat changes and the events which produce them again depends upon your interpretation.

Point of concentration   To reveal the *events* which promote the major shifts in the scene's energy and direction.

ILLUSTRATION 1
Beat 1 of Anna Petrovna's scene culminates in her successfully prohibiting Platanov from dismissing their passionate past, for he says no more.

Because of that event, she then, in Beat 2, enlists the forces of nature, which charge the atmosphere surrounding them with a pure energy. Her actions cause an intimacy between them to be rekindled, which Platanov struggles to avoid. At the end of this Beat she touches her finger to his lips in an attempt to retain the purity and potency of their moment. This she achieves.

Because of *this* event, in Beat 3 she can now speak with extreme candour. She consequently offers him an escape back to what they once shared, but she sees this only depresses him, as he views her suggestion as fruitless and impossible.

Because of *this* event, she states in Beat 4 that she will leave him forever, forlorn and lost. She therefore proposes that he take all that life has to offer. She concludes they both love each other and nothing could be simpler. This event affects him in that she is reaching him and he can perhaps resist no longer.

In the final and most important Beat, Anna Petrovna now reveals her fragility and vulnerability. She concludes that this special moment is for them, that they must live, and that their relationship must be reborn so as to save them. The main event of the scene is that he agrees, and as the fireworks explode across the night sky, they exit into the shadows of the forest.

Each beat culminates in an *event* — something *happens* which alters the energy and direction of the scene. A journey becomes clear as we have revealed the structure behind the lines and can now release each beat's fullest potential. In essence, we have deciphered the overall score of the scene.

Notice that I haven't used words which emotionally charge the choices: Anna Petrovna *exclaims*, she *suggests*, she *offers*, she *clarifies*, she *expounds*, she *invokes*, she *concludes*. I haven't entered into *how* she goes about doing these things. That's for you to discover through your rehearsal. How *provocative, dismissive, challenging, seductive* she is depends upon your interpretation.

ILLUSTRATION 2

Following are three more examples of speeches divided into their beats.

Firstly, read Bubba's speech from Ray Lawler's *Summer of the Seventeenth Doll*. She talks to Roo and Barney after the drama and conflict of the preceding night. Dowdie has asked her out and she tells the two men for the first time of her true feelings and needs.

BUBBA: *It's no use tryin' to talk me out of it, Roo... He sent you out of the room and told me not to... to take any notice of what you said.* ①

Then he asked me... He asked me! And he didn't call me B-Bubba or kid, he wanted to know what my real name was, and when I told him, that's what he called me. Kathie. ②

[She turns away to ROO.]

He might have been drinking, and this morning he might have forgotten like you said, but this is the only chance I've ever had of comin' close to — I dunno — whatever it is I've been watching all these years. You think I'll give that up?... ③

Dolls and breaking things, and — and arguments about who was ④
best — what do they all matter? That wasn't the lay-off... | *I'll have*
what you had — the real part of it — but I'll have it differently. ⑤
Some way I can have it safe and know that it's going to last... | *No*
matter what happens, I'll always remember you, 'n' this house, 'n' ⑥
the lay-off.

Now that you've read the scene and seen the six beats as I have marked them, choose each beat's *key phrase* — the phrase without which the beat would lose its focus, drive and meaning. This will give you a strong insight into the plot or action of the beat and of course, its function. Do this exercise for yourself before reading on.

Here are the key lines as I interpret them: Beat 1 - *No use*; Beat 2 - *He asked me!*; Beat 3 - *the only chance*; Beat 4 - *What do they matter?*; Beat 5 - *That's going to last*; Beat 6 - *I'll always remember you.*

If you have chosen effectively, the six key phrases when read together should tell the story of the speech by themselves — they should distil the essential meaning and chart the speeches journey. Each key phrase should also relate to every line *within* the beat — in other words, your chosen key phrase represents the main idea driving that beat, and all other lines surrounding it shape that idea.

Look at the following speech from *Henry VI – Part One*. Joan la Pucelle visits Charles with a very clear objective in mind. The speech has four beats — each one becomes a building block in which Joan attempts to change the Dauphin's will by leading him towards her vision of how things could be.

JOAN:
Dolphin, I am by birth a shepherd's daughter,
My wit untrained in any kind of art.
Heaven and our Lady gracious hath it please   ①
To shine on my contemptible estate.

Lo, whilst I waited on my tender lambs,
And to sun's parching heat displayed my cheeks,
God's mother deigned to appear to me,
And in a vision, full of majesty,   ②
Willed me to leave my base vocation
And free my country from calamity.
Her aid she promised, and assured success.

In complete glory she revealed herself —
And whereas I was black and swart before,
With those clear rays which she infused on me   ③
That beauty am I blest with, which you may see.

Ask me what question thou canst possible,
And I will answer unpremeditated.
My courage try by combat, if thou dar'st,
And thou shalt find that I exceed my sex.   ④
Resolve on this: thou shalt be fortunate,
If thou receive me for they warlike mate.

This time I have given each beat a title — it works in a similar way to the key phrase — the title sums up the main idea which fuels the beat. It also serves as a reminder as to exactly what the other person must *understand* if you are indeed to change their mind and therefore achieve your objective.

Beat 1; *I have been chosen*. Beat 2; *I had a vision of freedom - victory*. Beat 3; *I am transformed*. Beat 4; *Our crusade begins!*

An excellent rehearsal technique is to repeat the title of the beat after each line of the text (using major punctuation as your guide, *ie* a full-stop, exclamation mark, colon, semi-colon and question mark). You will find this a very effective way in which to charge each line with an energy and focus its impact. It will invest meaning and give you an aim to everything you say and do onstage, *ie*:

> *Dolphin, I am by birth a shepherd's daughter,*
> *My wit untrained in any kind of art.*
> *Yet I have been chosen!*
> *Heaven and our Lady gracious hath it pleased*
> *To shine on my contemptible estate.*
> *I have been chosen!!*

Choose whatever title propels you into action. Use any words which catapult you away from 'inventing' in order to be correct, towards an organic connection to the reality of who you are and what you are there to do.

Lastly, look at Rosalind's speech from *As You Like It*. Once again, four very clear beats. Once you are clear on the sense of the speech — which will mean a line by line literal translation — look at the beat titles. Use the title after each line of the text and observe how they empower the words, shaping ideas and making every moment of the scene a movement into the future. (Remember: use major punctuation).

ROSALIND:
And why, I pray you? Who might be your mother,
'That you insult, exult, and all at once,
Over the wretched? What though you have no beauty —
As, by my faith, I see no more in you   ①
Than without candle may go dark to bed —
Must you be therefore proud and pitiless?
_____
Why, what means this? Why do you look on me?
I see no more in you than in the ordinary
Of nature's sale-work. — Odd's my little life,
I think she means to tangle my eyes, too!   ②
No, faith, proud mistress, hope not after it.
'Tis not your inky brows, your black silk hair,
Your bugle eyeballs, nor you cheek of cream,
That can entame my spirits to your worship.
_____
[To SILVIUS] You, foolish shepherd, wherefore do you follow her
Like foggy south, puffing with wind and rain?
You are a thousand times a properer man
Than she a woman. 'Tis such fools as you

> *That makes the world full of ill-favoured children.* ③
> *'Tis not her glass but you that flatters her,*
> *And out of you she sees herself more proper*
> *Than any of her lineaments can show her.*

> [TO PHEBE] *But, mistress, know yourself; down on your knees*
> *And thank heaven, fasting, for a good man's love;*
> *For I must tell you friendly in you ear,*
> *Sell when you can. You are not for all markets.* ④
> *Cry the man mercy, love him, take his offer;*
> *Foul is most foul, being foul to be a scoffer. —*
> *So, take her to thee, shepherd. Fare you well.*

Beat 1; You are so full of pride and arrogance! Beat 2; I can't give you anything you desire! Beat 3; Don't be a fool for love! Beat 4; Wake up and smell the coffee!!!

Now we want to *further* seek out what is possible. The preparation has been done, the launching pad is secure; our exploration continues.

EXERCISE 3: Explore and Heighten

This exercise derives from a Viola Spolin exercise. Once again I have adapted the concept to text. It was developed as a tool to help release particular emotional dynamics from an improvisation.

Explanation After the improvisation, the teacher suggests the scene be re-enacted but this time the actors are asked to develop, as often as possible, *one aspect* of the scene. For example, if the scenario is a first date, then whenever possible, *explore* through the scene, then *heighten* whenever possible, the embarrassment, the sexual attraction, the need to impress, or indeed the silences. Once heightened, each element brings a different dimension to the scene. Through this exploratory work you will find aspects which release the scene's dramatic essence.

Application This exercise can be used as effectively with text. You might find the dynamics arising from your exploration suddenly suit the words and the interaction. As a result, you may have moved one step closer to revealing the playwright's intentions. As opposed to Extend/Advance, which deals with specific word/idea meaning, this exercise focuses on the particular *issues* which certain beats reveal. It also offers us the chance to probe particular dimensions of the character's emotional condition.

Point of concentration To allow the chosen dimension being explored to impact upon the beat, and for this aspect to be released through the scene's action.

ILLUSTRATION 1
You can choose to explore and heighten any element you feel will help release the scene's life and extend its range. With the previous scene from *Wild Honey*, you could embrace and amplify any of the following: Anna Petrovna's recklessness, passion, intimacy, seductiveness, innocence, manipulation, loneliness, desperation, sexual prowess.

With your beats chosen, elect *one* beat and explore a particular, and perhaps appropriate, dimension. After looking at the dimension of the character I have chosen to heighten below, keep it clear in your mind while you re-read the corresponding beat and observe any changes which occur.

Beat 1: Amplify her defiance. (Now read Beat 1.)
Beat 2: Amplify her magnetism.
Beat 3: Amplify her sensual potency.
Beat 4: Amplify her appetite for the reckless.
Beat 5: Amplify her hunger for all life has to offer.

This exploration should reveal what drives the beat. But it may also prove ineffective and therefore point your search in another direction. Or you may find it releases exactly the right energy for the scene on only a *few* of the lines. This is precisely what the rehearsal period is for — provoking what's possible, pushing the boundaries of the character's expression, plunging into the depths of the scene's dynamic range.

Theatre is the result of a collision of values. Through this collision we gain insight and understanding. [17]

Use *Explore and Heighten* to pinpoint, then provoke each of the character's values or issues which collide head-on in each beat. For example: Beat 1 — her truth *vs* his fabrication; Beat 2 — her intimacy *vs* his sense of responsibility; Beat 3 — her passion *vs* his fear; Beat 4 — her freedom *vs* his restraint; Beat 5 — her surrender *vs* his temptation which leads to acceptance.

Because acting is the passionate pursuit of an objective, obstacles can therefore produce great passion.

The issues above highlight the many obstacles Anna Petrovna has to deal with. These issues provide potent stimuli within the speech which you can react off. They provoke *actions* which lead to developing the score of the speech.

Remember to allow the dimension you are heightening to be revealed through this interaction and not merely tacked on as an emotional state or characteristic. It doesn't mean Anna's character is *powerful* throughout the beat, but there will be moments when her strength of will and purpose will become active and dominant and she is able to affect powerful change in Platanov. The chosen aspect *translates* into action. Once again, don't play the effect: connect to its cause.

ILLUSTRATION 2

Some frequently performed speeches, like Hamlet's *'O, what a rogue and peasant slave am I!'*, are often done with one characteristic dominating the scene. As such, the entire text swims in an emotional wash of either seething anger, uncontrolled rage, mild philosophical musing or a maudlin and inactive depression. The actor begins by taking a deep breath then proceeds to, very successfully, explore and heighten *one aspect* of the character's world. This limits the scene's range and inhibits the dynamics possible. But through uncovering the beats in the scene, you may find the above mentioned aspects *all* appear in some form at some stage.

Hamlet has moments where he abases himself and despises his inactivity. He then tries to comprehend his predicament. From here he attempts to take the path of direct, positive action. But more the fool he, for he discovers that this path alludes him. As a result of his inability to act, the pressures become a battle where he hits out at the world at large for thinking him a coward. He then acknowledges his lack of courage and inner weakness. Through his emotional miasma he makes the dilemma surrounding him concrete and elucidates what exactly should be done. He rails to the gods and calls forth his only ally and saviour, *'O, vengeance!'*

Discover firstly the beats, then uncover what is peculiar to each beat. In other words, what function does it serve? To help find this out, ask what the speech would lose if the beat were to be cut? You'll soon see what purpose it serves and that will give you powerful clues as to what your rehearsal needs to focus on.

ILLUSTRATION 3
In later rehearsals you may want to explore and heighten aspects of the scene other than those already mentioned. For example:

• the pre-life to the scene — what has just affected the character.
• the discoveries the character makes (see EXERCISE 6).
• the inner tension or preoccupation the character may be experiencing.
• the conditions which surround the character, such as the temperature and other climactic elements.
• the setting — forest, beach, boardroom. Each environment can have is own effect on the scene.
• the knowledge that someone may overhear or indeed enter.
• the conflict.
• the dilemma.
• the potency of the inner monologue (see EXERCISE 4).
• the impact of the events.

All of these dimensions can contribute to your onstage reality and create atmosphere. They offer various dynamics which can inform your acting and help release the scene's depth and quality. You can now choose what works and plot it in as part of the scene's journey.

Allow *Explore and Heighten* to stimulate your imagination and provide an arena for your creative exploration of the issues driving each beat. The result will be a strong and vivid belief in all you do and your speech will show an extensive range of the character's emotional life.

EXERCISE 4: Inner Monologue/Departures

Application If we could record on a disk someone's inner thoughts — his or her most intimate reactions, second by second, to all he or she encountered, and if this disc was to be lodged in *our* nerve centre, we would know what it is to *be* someone else. To embrace another's inner perception in this deeply subjective way would lead us to the inner core of his or her being and reveal the person's psyche. As a result, we would experience the *sensations* from which spring all the person says and does.

This is also the realm from which a *character's* reality is formed. Obviously then, it will be advantageous to us as actors to inhabit a character's inner thoughts — in essence, to *think* as the character would, not as the actor.

It is always interesting to observe the actor's degree of such internal focus on an opening night. No matter how skilled the 'performance' of the role, letters passed onstage shake, brims of hats quiver, any intricate action requires extra concentration. Hence the lighting of a cigarette, an ordinary daily activity performed with little thought, suddenly demands dexterity and a high level of skill. On that all too important opening the actor's inner monologue affects the character's world.

But return to the production perhaps only a few performances later and a *fusion* has taken place: an actor/character melding of the internal and the external worlds. The character's deep inner thoughts and perceptions have been embraced by the *actor's* inner workings. All intricate action now appears totally natural, unconscious. The actor now seems to own and inhabit his or her onstage world with complete surety.

In an audition you do not have the luxury of a performance season to find this fusion. Therefore, your rehearsal period must at some point focus on the character's deep inner workings so that, under pressure, you can still feel released and at ease within your character's reality.

Explanation   This exercise contributes to the fusion referred to above. You can use it alone or someone else can be your side-coach. As before, have your script handy. Most of these rehearsal room exercises shake up what we know and enable us to discard old patterns. Trying to remember lines and what comes next are the last things you want to expend energy on.

Once again, concentrate your internal energies on the situation. Begin when you feel connected to your first need.

If you have someone working with you, he or she should direct you at some point during the speech to release *out loud* the character's inner thoughts *at that instant*. On the instruction 'Inner monologue', simply plug into that internal disc mentioned earlier and allow the character's deep subjectivity in that moment to fuel your departure. Experience the myriad of thoughts and sensations rocketing through the character's nervous system. It doesn't matter what you say — it's not poetry, nor does it even have to make sense. It is for no one's benefit but your own.

After somewhere between six and a dozen of your own lines, your side-coach should direct you to 'Play on'. At this point, return to the script and allow your next line to be *affected* by your inner monologue departure. Remember: The energy in the scene should now be *different*. Allow an inner journey to take place which will charge the scene ahead.

Point of concentration   To plug into and experience the character's deep subjective thinking process and to allow its vivid and muscular quality to affect the ensuing moment.

ILLUSTRATION 1
During Nina's speech to her psychiatrist in Anthony Minghella's screenplay, *Truly, Madly, Deeply*, she speaks about Jamie, her deceased fiance:

First read the dialogue in italics *only,* then include the inner monologue departure examples allowing them to affect your *re-reading* of the scene.

NINA
Mostly when I'm walking, at night, or anyway, alone, if I'm frightened, then he'll turn up...
Inner monologue: 'out of nowhere, suddenly *beamed-in* beside me... with that extraordinary familiarity... that feeling... affirming... he *knew* me completely. We had *recognition*. (Play on.)
...he'll, he'll talk, about what I'm doing...
Inner monologue: 'because you see I was scared, and always a bit of a klutz and he... he'd instruct me, that's how it felt, and it helped... he cared.' (Play on.)
...you know, some advice, he'll say — 'Don't be frightened. I've told you — walk in the middle of the road at night.
Inner monologue: 'He'd sort of lose patience with me, but he was joking. He had such kind eyes. Love does that.' (Play on.)

And I will, I move over to the middle of the road, or, I don't know, he'll say: 'It's a disgrace, this street is a disgrace, there's no proper lighting, have you written, you must write!'

Inner monologue: 'I'd love it when he became militant and wanted to change the world. He'd get all feisty and fired up. He pushed me from my safe-zone... challenged me. (Play on.)

He's always forthright, I mean he always was forthright so I suppose that's not, but, you know...

Inner monologue: 'Christ, the blackness — the wasteland — get it together! You can't go on, you haven't got the energy — search, speak more, find a new distraction...' (Play on.)

... he'll also speak in Spanish to me, which is odd because he couldn't speak Spanish —

Inner monologue: 'it's pointless remembering all this, it's like hot pokers slicing through my stomach, but... you must... deal with... how can I move on... I... don't lose it... keep going... face it...' (Play on.)

and I would be feeling low, you know, very alone and hopeless and — and then he's there, his presence, and it's okay, it's fine, and I don't mind and he tells me he loves me.

Inner monologue: 'I remember his lips — his eyelashes — when he spoke of love the air changed. The incredible *ease* I felt — unburdened and protected. I breathed fresh breath and seemed to *know* more.. He *became* my longing'. (Play on.)

And then he's not there any more.

Inner monologue: 'But it lasts — his touch. It stays within and sleeps with me for days. Stupid, I know. He knows just when the blackness... the void... descends... opens... he... just... knows, and...' (Play on.)

...I feel looked after, I suppose, watched over.

(Now re-read the dialogue *and* the inner monologue departures.)

Nina's *interior* world becomes a part of the scene's tapestry. Her public interaction and her private thoughts and feelings begin to work in tandem and the associations made on the departures empower the text. This works in a similar way to *Extend/Advance* but offers a greater scope for the broader, general thoughts surrounding the text. The departures can also develop strong atmospheric dynamics within the scene. The example above is only *one* interpretation. Each actor will embody the scene differently. It is this aspect of the inner monologue which will mark the speech as distinctly your own.

Note that there are two options you can take on your return:
1. Release the inner feelings you stirred during the departure.
2. Hide them and keep them as private thoughts.
Either way (and it may change from line to line as the speech progresses), allow the scene to *develop* and be *altered* in response to the specific inner dynamic with which you return.

ILLUSTRATION 2
For example, if in a scene you are not getting through to someone you might, on your departure, rant and rave and indulge in every obscenity you can conjure. Then, after the 'play on', you may smile and look completely rational and together, with not a care in the world — happy and content to once more state your case and work towards a resolution. But, as a result of your departure, as you begin to speak your *over*-politeness and *accentuated* genuineness tells the audience that something's got to give. Comedy in a scene is often heightened significantly when the pressure of the inner monologue is so great it requires containment. Even though you may choose to conceal your inner thoughts in this way, your departure has changed the energy and dynamic tension of the scene and therefore moved the scene forward.

The *Inner Monologue Departures* stir the sub-text — the thoughts behind the lines. They also assist you in discovering the life-blood of the character and creating an inner foundation from which the character's outer world can spring.

EXERCISE 5: 'Is This Good or Bad for Me?' [18]

Sometimes at an audition the comments from the panel focus on a similar theme: 'the actor didn't appear connected'; 'didn't work off the other actor'; 'skimmed across the surface'; 'it all seemed too performed and predictable'; 'it didn't engage me'.

One major factor often evident in auditions is the actor's inability to *process* the scene. Processing entails three stages:
1. Acknowledgment of the incoming stimulus, i.e. the other person's reaction, or an idea or thought you have just had.
2. Embracing that stimulus by attaching your attitude to it.
3. Amplifying the stimulus by choosing to react in a particular way which will affect change in the other person, or within yourself (if for example, doing a soliloquy).

The lack of processing can be a danger for actors during long runs. In such cases, the choices made, moment by moment, often become not choices but *decisions*, and are not provoked by incoming stimulus, but by a pre-learnt and rigid sequence of cues. Here, the actor has inadvertently disengaged from the very process of *choosing* what to do and how to react and is on 'automatic pilot'. The very word 'choice' implies *options*. This process may take only a split second but these options must be entertained before a decision can be reached. By committing to the three stages outlined above, it will lead the actor to being *in the moment* — often referred to as the 'here and now'.

In life we process automatically and every split second. Every stimulus that we register through our senses demands a response from us: a phone ringing, a knock at the door, everything said to us, the tone in a person's voice, the look in his or her eyes. Our response depends on whether what we smell, taste, touch, see or hear is ultimately going to be either good or bad for us. Once our attitude to the stimulus is formed, we have a basis from which to react. We make *conscious* choices. There are also many moments in our day when we react *unconsciously*, purely from instinct, but in this exercise we are concerned with the *conscious* decisions we make when there are options present.

Application The following exercise deals with this aspect of processing. It reminds you to stay in each and every moment and to continue the scene *only* after you have found a *reason* to go on.

I remember the director, Gale Edwards, working with a young actor in an audition. His nerves and desire to *get it right* led him to push through the scene and have little contact with the other character. His eyes seemed glazed as he *worked* the scene and tried to create the effect he was after.

Gale suggested he try the scene again but *this* time to find a reason *within the other character* before he continued on to his next line, i.e. to use the other character's *resistance, annoyance, confusion*, or *delight*.

It is the other character's reactions which can become your stimulus — your reason to go on. If you're not getting your desired result or reaction, try another way. If you *are* getting what you want, want *more*. In other words, rather than self-motivating, allow the other character's energy and reactions to be your fuel.

Gale's re-direction took a number of seconds for the actor to process. Up until this point he had been only aware of himself in action. In other words, his focus had been on the inner manufacturing of his emotions and then the external monitoring of their success.

The actor then went to re-enter the scene as he had done, but even here Gale asked him to begin the speech sitting opposite the other actor. In effect, she was releasing him from his set moves that were contributing to him following his pre-learnt sequence of cues.

She reminded him once again to find a reason *within the other actor* to fuel each line. Once understood, and almost immediately as he began, it was as if his sight had been restored — he made contact and dealt with the other actor's energy. He began crafting each idea in an effort to affect change. If the other actor turned away or actually *walked away,* this became a major event. We were now watching an exchange. Even though it was a monologue, it appeared to be a scene (as indeed *all* monologues are). The actor's processing engaged us step by step, moment by moment. His choices *became* choices, and not merely a rehearsed set of decisions.

The following exercise promotes this clear processing and places you firmly in the *here and now*.

Point of concentration To name the exact stimulus affecting you in the moment, and to then attach a *significant* emotional attitude towards that stimulus.

Explanation This can be done on your own or with another actor. After focusing on the scene and your initial need, say your first line. Then deal with whatever you *see* or *imagine* the other character to be doing or thinking and then, in your own words, process its meaning and relevance in terms of your immediate needs.

ILLUSTRATION 1
Let's take a simple first date scenario. You've had dinner, seen the movie, and are presently being dropped off outside your home. The car idles, your leather jacket seems to squeak uncontrollably as you try to decide, 'What next?':

First, read only the speech in italics, then re-read and include the inner processing.
    MAN: *What a cold night. I think winter's really on its way now.*

Is this good or bad for me? This is bad, she's looking bored. She's definitely lost interest. Her body seems sort of slumped. I've blown it.

I really enjoyed the movie. The ending was a real shock. I wasn't expecting it.

Is this good or bad for me? This is not just bad, it's pointless. She obviously hated the movie and predicted the ending within two minutes of the start. Her eyes have sort of glazed over now and her fingers are fidgeting like she's loosing patience. This is really bad for me.

Look, I'd better go — I've got some work to catch up on tonight. Thanks again.

Is this good or bad for me? I think it's good — I might be wrong — but she seems slightly disappointed. Her head has turned towards me and she has a slight look of expectation. This could be very good.

I'm up early tomorrow, you know, pretty busy... but... do you, maybe, want to come in for a coffee?

Is this good or bad for me? You bloody idiot! She seems unsure now and hesitant. She's checking her watch. Why did you have to leap into it? Relax. This is getting worse.

It's probably too late. And anyway, (yawning and checking his watch) *is that the time?* (She suddenly turns off the engine.)

Is this good or bad for me? This is becoming highly interesting for me! She looks like she wants to say something. Her head has leaned slightly to the side, her eyes have an expectant quality. Her lips have parted and just now have broken into a slight smile. This could be extraordinarily good!

The 'Is this good or bad for me?' question anchors you to the precise moment. You acknowledge the signals around you, assimilate their meaning, and then attach your attitude. You move into the next moment knowing *what* has just occurred, and *how* you feel towards it. What you choose to *do* because of it depends on the choices you feel are appropriate for the character and the scene.

Actors can become isolated in rehearsals if they place too much emphasis on trying to decide what choice would work best. It can lead them to a clinical search for the end result: 'What should my next moment be? What should the character do?'

I feel it's more beneficial to place your focus on the stimuli you *receive* from the other actor. Claim how *it* makes you feel, then allow yourself to *react*. The old adage that acting is reacting can at times sound too simple, but it offers invaluable advice. Give yourself the permission to *react*, based on your internal processing. Know how something makes you feel then let this sensation lead you to *action*. Discover the acting through the *re*acting.

ILLUSTRATION 2
Let's apply this exercise to a speech. In Louis Nowra's *Sunrise*, Irene talks about her fourteen-year-old daughter, Venice, and her relationship to her father. Irene sees her parents and extended family as disparate and estranged. They have all gathered for a reunion on their father's estate in the South Australian hills.

As before, read only Irene's *dialogue*. After you are familiar with the text, re-read *both* the dialogue *and* the character's inner processing.

IRENE: *She loves him very much.*
Is this good or bad for me? This is bad. Venice sees only the charming things in him, and offers herself to him in a way she never can with me. It's bitterly disappointing — to be loved less. (This is her inner stimulus which will now amplify into her next thought.)
One day I hope she'll go back to Africa and see him as he really is, a marvellous scholar who's gone troppo...
Is this good or bad for me? This memory is very painful. It cuts open my heart and tries to suffocate me. I have no marriage, I feel abandoned and blame myself. It's desolate.
He became so immersed in the language and culture of the people he studied that he became one of them. He used to take Venice to fetish markets — God they're disgusting; putrid smells, monkey heads, dog's teeth, gecko skins...
Is this good or bad for me? This is disturbing. The markets became an obsession. They fuelled his descent into madness. They drew him from me and left me isolated. This memory is painful.
He loved buying them. As souvenirs, he said; but he believed in their powers — Once, when I was in Paris, he took Venice to a tribe who wanted her to help break the drought, because she was white-skinned and blonde like their spirit ancestors...
Is this good or bad for me? This is very confronting. This was the moment I felt I was robbed of my daughter. She was taken from me, and I've been denied access ever since. It disempowered me forever. She was so frightened, so vulnerable. And I could do nothing.
Venice was covered in black grease. Geckos and a goat were

slaughtered and their blood poured over her — All the while Alex took pictures. You can see Venice's eyes in the photographs — such terror, such incomprehension! I'll never forgive him for that. She was only seven.

Is this good or bad for me? It is frightening. This was the moment I saw the 'shift' in her life. She would never be the same. I became furious, outraged — yet impotent...

And she still loves him. More than she loves me. Venice has no barriers between her and life. She's like a sponge that soaks up everything.

Is this good or bad for me? This is absolutely unnerving. She has no life-discrimination. She 'absorbs' the world and all its strangeness, daily withdrawing further. It's deeply distressing...

She's in a world I'm not allowed entry into. Even when she was born she had distant eyes. (Smiling) *But what can you expect coming from this background...*

Is this good or bad for me? This is ironic. Here I am again — back home — feeling like the incompetent child, being contaminated by all that surrounds me, undermined at every turn. It's depleting, maddening...

I don't know what I'm going to do with her, David. Sometimes I think she's a normal fourteen-year-old and then... other times I know she's touched.

Is this good or bad for me? It's terrifying. I stand by watching without any ability to affect change. I observe her 'disappearance' minute by minute and blame myself. But I blame more this mess around us and these people who taught us to hate ourselves.

This exercise shows *Irene's memories* to be her stimulus. These associations and all they trigger drive the speech. We see clearly the springboards from one thought to the next and the inner impulses which, once personalised, will allow the actor to *react*. Once this interior work has been specified the *scene* will begin to supply the emotional energy, not the actor. This is the ideal situation for any actor: to be surrounded by circumstances powerful enough to propel you into action, by motivating all you do and say.

The other situation where the exercise is of benefit is in the case of a speech where the dialogue springs from the character's *interaction* with another, such as in the scene from *Wild Honey* where Platanov's reactions, and the events which result, fuel all Anna Petrovna says. If each moment of the scene is not acknowledged, embraced then amplified, you'll end up acting in a void — inventing rather than responding.

ILLUSTRATION 3

Let's look at another play by Louis Nowra. *The Golden Age* tells the story of two young men who come across a lost tribe in the Tasmanian hills. In this scene, Francis follows one of the tribe members, Betsheb, to the river. She fascinates him, and his attraction to her leads him to make further contact.

Remember one of the essential principles in rehearsal is if you're not getting what you want moment by moment, try another way to get it. If you *are* getting what you want, *want* more. Observe this process in the following scene.

Once again, read *only* the dialogue and stage directions first.

[The river, twilight. Betsheb sits, staring out at the evening sun. Francis enters and watches her for some time.]

Is this good or bad for me? This is perfect. She's by herself. She seems calm and relaxed. Her eyes are haunted yet knowing. I must understand her. She holds secrets.

FRANCIS: *Are you looking at the sunset?* [Startled, Betsheb turns around.]

Is this good or bad for me? This is bad. She seems frightened. Her body has become alert. A fear burns in her eyes. She seems poised and prepared to run away. Mustn't lose this opportunity.

[Smiling] *I'm not a monster... No more running.*

Is this good or bad for me? This shows promise. She hasn't run. She's wary though, her hands still grip her thighs, but she seems prepared to test me out. I think this is good.

[Silence. He walks closer to the river.] *Look at us reflected in the water, see? Upside down.*

Is this good or bad for me? This is very good. She's allowed me to get much closer. She's less tense. She's looking in the water. Her face shows fascination by the image. She has become like a child. Relax her more. Calm her. Befriend her.

[He smiles and she smiles back. Silence.]

Is this good or bad for me? This is the most positive sign yet. She's letting me in. She's as curious of me as I am of her.

So quiet. I'm not used to such silence. I'm a city boy, born and bred.

Is this good or bad for me? This is quite strange. Her nostrils flare as if she's trying to smell my very thoughts. She wants to know more.

You've never seen a city or a town, have you? Where I live there are dozens of factories: shoe factories, some that make gaskets, hydraulic machines, clothing. My mother works in a shoe factory. [Pointing to his boots] *These came from my mother's factory.* [Silence.]

Is this good or bad for me? This is extraordinary. She seems transfixed. Unlike any creature I've ever encountered. Her body is supple and receives instinctive impulses. She disarms me — fascinates me. This world I've entered is provoking, haunting...

These sunsets here, I've never seen the likes of them. A bit of muddy orange light in the distance, behind the chimneys, is generally all I get to see.

Is this good or bad for me? This is very good. She smiled again. Her eyes have softened. She's more interested. Her hands play in the dirt and her head leans to the side. She likes me. She wants more.

You'd like the trams, especially at night. They rattle and squeak, like ghosts rattling their chains, and every so often the conducting rod hits a terminus and there is a brilliant spark of electricity, like an axe striking a rock. 'Spiss!'

Is this good or bad for me? This is great. She is completely alive. Her body responds to everything and she's locked in on my energy.

On Saturday afternoon thousands of people go and watch the football. A huge oval of grass. [Miming a football] *A ball like this. Someone hand passes it, 'whish', straight to me. I duck one lumbering giant, spin around a nifty dwarf of a rover, then I catch sight of the goals.*

Is this good or bad for me? This is fantastic. She is totally absorbed. She feeds off all I do and say.

I boot a seventy-yard drop kick straight through the centre. The crowd goes wild! [He cheers wildly. Betsheb laughs at his actions. He is pleased to have made her laugh.]

As you see, the actor's inner processing becomes clear: you acknowledge the stimulus, assimilate its meaning, and then allow your *reaction* to propel the scene forward. This detailed work leads you to inhabit fully the character's moment-by-moment onstage reality. It is this detail which leads the audience through the scene's journey and allows them access to the stage experience.

As a very revealing exercise, watch an international interview on television. Due to the split-second delay as the signals bounce around in outer space, you are privy to a moment normally missed. Because we process so quickly, when viewing a *local* interview we are caught up with our own processing of the question and miss the initial impact on the interviewee. But because of the time delay in an international interview, that precious split second is revealed — we have already ascertained whether *we* regard the question's impact as good or bad, so are afforded the luxury of witnessing that precise moment when the person on the receiving end does the same. The more tricky or con-fronting the question the more accentuated this moment will become.

Use 'Is this good or bad for me?' whenever you wish to clarify the moment-by-moment interaction. It reveals inner motivation and amplifies the choice-making process, engaging the audience on a fundamental and essential level.

EXERCISE 6: Major Discovery

Application As we have mentioned in the previous exercise, in life we continually deal with our ever-changing environment second by second. Every stimulus received is either hostile or friendly. When translated to the stage, these spontaneous discoveries becomes highly engaging for an audience for they parallel our daily life experience. Watching people 'change', being affected and having to deal with continually mutating sensory information, fascinates us. Life consists of this. Our stage life concentrates and distils this process, providing life-parallels and therefore, a mirror to nature — the essence of the theatre experience.

Great plays are written around great conditions.[19]

You must fully activate your character's sense of *discovery* in order to highlight these great conditions and their effect on you. This will lead to a spontaneous stage life where your awareness of your acting is dissolved and you surrender to the offers around you, and once again, *react.*

Point of concentration To acknowledge every discovery possible in the speech, and to then transform that discovery into *physical* action.

Explanation You will need some room around you in which to move — the larger the space the better.

Allow each discovery the character makes to motivate a physical move somewhere in the space — a run, a turn, a swift walk in a particular direction. In other words, release the emotional revelation through a *physical* impulse.

ILLUSTRATION 1

In Shakespeare's play *All's Well That Ends Well*, Helena has fallen in love with the Countess' son, Bertram. He then departs for the wars without any knowledge of Helena's feelings towards him. After he has gone, Lafew, a courtier, and the Countess see Helena in distress and attribute this to the recent death of her father. They suggest she try to overcome her mourning. They then exit, leaving her alone.

First, simply read the *dialogue*, which is in italics. Then read both the dialogue *and* the discoveries.

> LAFEW: *Farewell, pretty lady: you must hold the credit of your father.* [He and the Countess exit.]
> HELENA:

Discovery: They think I mourn for my father — crazy — no one knows my secret pain!! (Commit to a physical impulse.)

> *O, were that all! I think not on my father,*
> *And these great tears grace his remembrance more*
> *Than those I shed for him.*

Discovery: This is extraordinary — perhaps cruel and abnormal — I am crying more now than I did at my father's graveside!

> *What was he like? I have forgot him...*

Discovery: I can't believe this — my father's face, his eyes, the tone of his voice — I can't remember any of it.

> *... my imagination carries no favour in't but Bertram's.*

Discovery: All is truly lost — I have fallen far deeper than I ever realised — my heart and soul ache for only one person — and he is gone.

> *I am undone; there is no living, none,*
> *If Bertram be away;*

Discovery: This is so typical of me — to fall for someone I cannot have and who, if they knew, would surely *never* desire me.

> *'twere all one*
> *That I should love a bright particular star*

And think to wed it, he is so above me.
Discovery: Face it Helena, he is gone — all you have once again is your memories to live on.
In his bright radiance and collateral light
Must I be comforted, not in his sphere.
Discovery: But this won't work — I feel driven, I have little control over what I do or feel— destiny beckons — what to do?!!
The ambition in my love thus plagues itself;
The hind that would be mated by the lion
Must die for love.
Discovery: There is obviously *nothing* to be done — I must needs be consumed by my pain, devoured by my longing. Treasure the fantasy.
'Twas pretty, though a plague,
To see him every hour; to sit and draw
His arched brows, his hawking eye, his curls,
In our heart's table...
Discovery: You made yourself too vulnerable — big mistake — it only ever ends up like this — you cared too much — again.
— heart too capable
Of every line and trick of his sweet favour.
Discovery: You're getting maudlin now — get over it! You have no choice, you can do nothing, get on with your... lonely... life.
But now he's gone, and my idolatrous fancy
Must sanctify his relics.

For the above example I *articulated* each discovery, in a similar way to the inner monologue exercise. The difference here though is that the discovery isn't a verbalised one, but should be expressed through a major and vivid *energy production*. There needs to be a strong and powerful energy impulse produced in *reaction* to the discovery. If you only *think* the discovery you can end up acting purely *between* the lines rather than *on* the line. Better to allow the physical energy produced by the discovery to catapult you *into* the line, making the dialogue not only essential to the experience but also inevitable (see Plates 6 & 7).

When the Countess and Lafew exit, don't *think* about Helena's discovery, intuitively and impulsively *react, physically*. For example, walk away, sink to your knees, turn sharply away from the door. When she discovers she cannot remember her own father, don't *think* how she would feel, *react* — *create potent physical sensations*. For

77

example, run six metres as if hounded by the discovery, move towards your father's study, placing your hands and forehead against the door. When you discover how impossible your situation is, stand on your toes, reach towards the cosmos, attempt to touch what you cannot possess.

The consequence of what happens to you must be extreme and profound, otherwise you will give us superficial behaviour.[20]

Through embracing the scene's discoveries in a profoundly *physical* way, the depth and resonance of their meaning become more potent. In the end you may wish to stage Helena's speech standing stock still. But, as with the example we looked at earlier of the photograph album, once the sensation has been experienced, it is forever recorded. These inner impulses will drive the speech and surface in many significant and subtle ways.

By using this exercise I often find that when actors return from their physical exploration of the discoveries and stand to deliver their speech, their acting becomes simple yet clear, their expression more fluid, more lyrical, and their voices often reflect the enormous range they physically experienced moments earlier.

Use *Major Discovery* to unearth the physical impact of the scene's discoveries and therefore events. This will help release your inner impulses and create a dynamic journey for the scene.

EXERCISE 7: Choice of Impact

Explanation The object of this exercise is to entertain the various options for ideas which might fuel each line of text. More importantly, it allows you to focus on the desired *impact* of your lines.

Application We have mentioned before the difference between *sense* and *meaning*: sense being what is stated on the line, meaning being its desired *impact* on the receiver. (If the character is talking to themselves, ascertain what *part* of themselves they are trying to affect — i.e. what aspect of their nature are they attempting to change?) It *is meaning* which directs the audience's attention to the play's interpretation and vision, for the meaning encompasses significance and consequence.

Point of concentration To allow each idea option to be your sole focal point and motivation when you return and commit to the line of text.

ILLUSTRATION 1

In a scene-study class we were working on Sam Shepard's *Fool For Love*. At one point in the text, Eddie, May's lover and half-brother, rises from the table and says to her, 'I'll go'. Upon asking the actor what was the meaning behind his line, he responded, 'Just, I'll go, I guess'. We then looked at some other options:

I'll go and you will be the loser.
I'll go, but tell me to stay.
I'll go, but *don't* ask me to come back.
I'll go; I won't cause any more trouble.
I'll go, and within two hours you'll be on your knees begging me to return.
I'll go, you've really blown it this time, May.
I'll go, and I wouldn't stay if you pleaded with me.
I'll go, but tell me why it should end this way?

Each different idea option shapes the choice and is called a *transaction* — someone or something causing an effect on another. Each *line* becomes a transaction and, as such, must be crafted to achieve its desired result. The options listed above all craft that moment in the play differently and determine the meaning being presented to the audience.

There are 3838 lines in the play *Hamlet*. Every one of them could be counted as a transaction. *Therefore*, each of the 3838 stimuli fuelling the transactions must initially be acknowledged, then processed, and then the actor must release into the play an *energy impulse*. This is the definition of a play: 'an energy moving though time'.[21] As each moment passes through each actor, the play's journey is affected. The energy is either suppressed or supported, diverted or amplified. This process weaves the play's texture and creates the audience's journey. In essence, this moving energy houses the total theatre experience. How this energy is crafted is therefore extremely important.

The *sense* driving the energy impulses becomes the play's *infrastructure*. How each section of this scaffolding is to be *presented to* and *viewed by* the audience depends upon the *meaning* invested in it.

ILLUSTRATION 2

In Barry Levinson's *Diner*, Shrieve confronts his girlfriend Beth about playing his precious record collection. His first line is: 'You've been playing my records again'. Leaving aside for the moment the state of their relationship and what has just occurred, say the above line for sense. That is, Shrieve discovers his records are out of order and states his belief that Beth has been playing them.

Now, with your hand or some paper, cover the ten options listed below. When you're ready, reveal the options one by one, connecting to the idea. Then repeat the line from the play, allowing each individual option to affect the *impact* you wish to create.

> Option 1: *I can't believe it — after all I've asked you.* (Repeat line — 'You've been playing my records again'.)
>
> Option 2: *I am so disappointed in you.*
>
> Option 3: *This makes me so angry!*
>
> Option 4: *I'm warning you for the last time.*
>
> Option 5: *It's no big deal, I just need to know.*
>
> Option 6: *This is a joke, right?*
>
> Option 7: *You do this deliberately to upset me.*
>
> Option 8: *I'm trying very hard to control myself at this moment.*
>
> Option 9: *This time I've caught you red-handed.*
>
> Option 10: *This is just not fair.*

Now, evaluate how effective you feel you were in surrendering to each journey the line undertook. To what extent did you monitor and try to achieve the correct 'sound' you felt the line should have had?

The more you allow yourself to *react* to the specific attitude behind each option, the more effective you will be. If your focus falls onto trying to get the 'acting' right, self-consciousness sets in and your pure connection to each idea will be contaminated. If you organically connect to the precise stimulus (cause) and forget about its packaged effect (result) your *reaction* to the stimulus does the acting for you.

Remember: *attitude* is how you feel, *action* is what you do because of it. Each option gives you a clue as to how the character *feels*: i.e. disappointed, outraged, frustrated. You're *reaction* houses your action: i.e. to shock, confront, tease, undermine, shame. *This* is what will propel the scene forward and create drama.

ILLUSTRATION 3

In Shakespeare's *The Winter's Tale*, Hermione is accused by her husband Leontes of adultery. She is arrested and thrown into prison. Upon giving birth to a child believed not to be her husband's, she is brought before the people in the city square to await the Oracle's decision on her fate. She stands facing Leontes who once again accuses her.

HERMIONE: *Sir, spare your threats.*

As we did earlier, cover the options below and reveal them when you are ready. Actors are often reminded not to learn *words*, but *ideas*. With each of the following options, connect to the *idea* it presents and allow this to inform the line:

Option 1: *Please, no more false lies.*
Option 2: *I have no strength left to deny these claims.*
Option 3: *You small-minded fool.*
Option 4: *I know you are misguided and pray for your redemption.*
Option 5: *Do you honestly believe I fear anything of what you say?*
Option 6: *I will not be accused another time!*
Option 7: *If only you knew the destruction you have unleashed.*

When you come to perform your piece the ideas driving the lines will be 'known'. In other words, because of your rehearsal work the ideas will become part of the text, for you can't think one line whilst saying another. The same applies to the inner monologue work we have done. Once the sensations have been fully explored and given their voice, they too become 'known'. They condense and crystallise and become a deeper motivation than can be articulated. When onstage, you feed off this powerful, subterranean source. Once stored, your sense memory retains the galaxy of these sensations. They will be released when triggered by your body experiencing the action and through your verbal commitment to the text. Trust the words, trust the action.

Once you have the process working, ask someone who is familiar with the piece to offer you various options after each line. Don't concern yourself as to their appropriateness; your rehearsal journey will help align the choices that work and this will create your score.

Further Exercises

Listed below are a number of exercises which provide more opportunities for you to discover what may indeed be possible in your chosen scene.

1. Perform your speech within a time limit (45 or 60 seconds) and discover what dynamics emerge and may be appropriate given this sense of urgency.

2. Do your speech at the bedside of a dying person. Allow the thoughts to be informed by this intimate and fragile situation.

3. Build a strong physical activity into your speech: play sport, stack chairs, shadowbox, exercise. Allow these new and active physical impulses to impact upon the ideas.

4. Wash the dishes and imagine the character you are talking to is in the next room. See which words and thoughts become important and in which moments you seek a response.

5. Sit in a chair and close your eyes. Connect to the environment of the speech — the colours, textures, temperature, time, terrain. Allow your personal connections to all the images that build the atmosphere surrounding you to emerge.

6. Build your environment or, if possible, find a place which captures the essence of your speech's experience.

7. Work with another actor: do your speech to them knowing they want to leave the room. This they may begin to do at any time. Use the language to keep their attention.

8. Whilst working with another person, allow them to say, 'And again' anytime they wish a thought was clearer or an image more sharply defined. They may 'And again' you several times on the one line. The 'And again' doesn't request more volume or emphasis, but asks the intention to be clarified, i.e. the meaning and its impact.

9. Stand with your heels and the back of your head resting against a wall. Without moving your arms or head in any way, go through your speech in a whisper. Avoid pushing from the throat — allow your breath to flow easily. Your brain activity will become sharper and the thoughts highly concentrated.

10. As above, but imagine the person you are talking to is twenty-five feet away. Once again, allow your hands, arms and head to remain unengaged — let the thoughts and ideas cover the distance now using voice — watch the words come alive.

11. Choose a beat from your speech: take one thought from your *inner monologue* which you feel drives that beat and repeat it after each line. (see page 59 — *As You Like It.*)

   For example, in Act 1, Scene 5 of *Hamlet*, the ghost visits his son. Lines 15 to 20 could be fuelled by the following inner monologue: 'Listen and believe!!!'

Now, repeat this after each phrase of the following text:

   Ghost: I could a tale unfold whose lightest word
      would harrow up thy soul, (*Listen and believe!*)
   freeze thy young blood, (*Listen and believe!!*)
   Make thy two eyes like stars start from their spheres,
      (*Listen and believe!!*)
   Thy knotted and combined locks to part,
      (*Listen and believe!!!*)
   And each particular hair to stand on end
      Like quills upon the fretful porpentine.
      (*Listen and believe!!!!!!*)

Make up whatever line you feel propels you into the particular essence of the beat. These lines can be as simple as you like: *It's not fair/ She's so beautiful/ I will not stand for it any longer/ Listen to every word I say/ You must believe me/ Come with me now/ Trust in what I say.* Choose an appropriate phrase to repeat, one which informs the text and pinpoints the essential energy driving the beat. This exercise can be enormously stimulating as it invigorates the needs by making them very immediate. It also focuses your attention very much on changing the *will* of the person to whom you are transmitting the ideas — the essence of acting.

All of the examples in this book will hopefully work as triggers to help activate and illuminate your personal process. Each discovery you make will build your craft and lead to a stronger sense of artistry in all you do. Allow yourself to work with courage and conviction. Enjoy the expedition!

To accomplish great things, we must not only act but also dream, not only plan but also believe.

Notes

1) Michael Saint-Denis, *Training For The Theatre*, 1982, Theatre Arts Books, New York.
2) Constantin Stanislavsky, *My Life in Art*, 1980, Methuen, London.
3) Lisle Jones, Head of Theatre, West Australian Academy of Performing Arts.
4) Constantin Stanislavsky, *An Actor Prepares*, 1937, Geoffrey Bless Publishers, London.
5) Constantin Stanislavsky: quoted in Jean Benedetti, *Stanislavsky – An Introduction*, 1982, Methuen, London.
6) C.R. Rogers, 'Towards a Theory of Creativity': included in P.E. Vernon (ed.), *Creativity*, Penguin, London.
7) *ibid.*
8) *ibid.*
9) Stanislavsky, *Collected Works (Vol. IV): Stanislavsky's Legacy*
10) Viola Spolin, *Improvisation for the Theatre*, 1983, Northwestern University Press, USA.
11) *ibid.*
12) *ibid.*
13) Constantin Stanislavsky: quoted in Jean Benedetti, *Stanislavsky – An Introduction*, 1982, Methuen, London.
14) Stephane Mallarme: quoted in Michel Saint-Denis, *Training for the Theatre*, 1982, Theatre Arts Books, New York.
15) Michael Chekhov, *Lessons for the Professional Actor*, 1985, Performing Arts Journal Publications, New York.
16) Arthur Miller
17) Jerzy Grotowski, *Towards a Poor Theatre*, 1968, Methuen, London.
18) Yevgeny Lanskroi
19) Larry Hecht
20) Michael Shurtleff
21) Robert Benedetti

Select Reading List

Brian Bates, *The Way of the Actor*, 1986, Century Books, London.

Robert Benedetti, *The Actor at Work*, 1985, Prentice-Hall, Englewood Cliffs, NJ.

Robert Benedetti, *The Director at Work*, 1970, Prentice-Hall, Englewood Cliffs, NJ.

Patricia Bosworth, *Diane Arbus*, 1984, Avon Books, New York.

Michael Chekhov, *Lessons for the Professional Actor*, 1985, Performing Arts Journal Publications, New York.

Michael Chekhov, *To The Actor*, 1953, Harper and Row, New York.

Shauna Crowley, *The Screen Test Handbook*, 1990, Currency Press, Sydney.

Rollo May, *The Courage to Create*, 1976, Bantam Books, New York.

Michel Saint-Denis, *Training for the Theatre*, 1982, Theatre Arts Books, New York.

Viola Spolin, *Improvisation for the Theatre*, 1983, Northwestern University Press, USA.

Constantin Stanislavsky, *An Actor's Handbook* (edited and translated by Elizabeth Hapgood), 1963, Theatre Arts Books, New York.

P.E. Vernon (ed.), *Creativity*, Penguin, London.

PLATE 7
Uncovering physical impulses behind the thought. Actor, Hugh Jackman.

PLATE 8
The Journey Students at the Actor's Centre in their presentation of *Lulu*.
Directed by Ross McGregor. Movement design by Chrissie Koltai.

PLATE 9
'Why bring him here? A storm's coming... He wants to die outside.' W.A. Academy students in Louis Nowra's *The Golden Age*. Directed by Dean Carey.

PLATE 10
'Then have him! Go on, clear out with your soulmate!' Lisa Bailey and
Damian Pike as Jeanne and Jim from Betty Roland's *The Touch of Silk*.
Directed by Dean Carey

PART THREE

The
Monologues

The speeches in the following section offer an extensive selection of audition choices for the actor in training or the actor already working in the profession.

Most are highly suitable for the *General Audition,* where the speech is required to provide range, journey, impact. They present many opportunities for you to explore a wide expressive range.

Other speeches make themselves available for the *Specific Audition,* where you are auditioning for a particular role or type of character. These speeches offer equally strong dynamics but in a more defined and specific form. Their inner landscape may cover less terrain but when fully inhabited, a particular aspect of your abilities will be highlighted and showcased.

You will notice the following icon [★] applied to particular speeches. This denotes that the piece is also suitable for film/TV screen tests where the language needs to be appropriate to this particular audition situation. Still rich in range, these selections promote a more concentrated focus making them ideal for the medium in which they will be viewed. Some are indeed too long, but an edited section would be ideal

I have not classified the speeches under the usual headings of serious, comic, 'serio-comic', and so on. Although such classification might make the speeches easier to locate, I want to avoid influencing your interpretation by predetermining the approach. The scope of a speech is as wide as you wish it.

Please bear in mind that many of the speeches have been edited to create monologues of the right length and so that they give sufficient information to create the 'scene' or context from which they came. When you choose your selections, they should be rehearsed with reference to the complete text. Even if you decide to change the circumstances, please consult the original and complete source. Only should this reference point inform your decisions.

Some speeches are, in fact, too long for the purpose but are valuable to work on without necessarily intending to perform them. How long should a speech be? When conducting a class at The Actors' Centre, Michael Shurtleff, author of *Audition,* said that every speech he has ever *seen* has been too long! I feel that approximately forty-five seconds to one minute for a screen test, and between two and 2½ minutes for a theatre audition, provides a happy medium for all concerned.

LIST OF MONOLOGUES

Australia and New Zealand

Britain and Europe

USA

★ = MONOLOGUES SUITABLE FOR FILM/TV SCREEN TESTS.

Cheapside

David Allen   Currency, Sydney 1984

Scene 2

BALL:

[*He sets the scene, and then acts out the following with all the exuberance of the natural performer . . . very fast*]

Ma Bull's, midday, Mr Greene venturing forth for a pissy writers' lunch with fellow scribblers Mr Nashe and Mr Kyd – them buying 'cos of his dire straits – him getting stuck into the pickled herrings to which he's more than partial (very fartable, your pickled herring!) washed down with plenty of [*tippling motion*] you know . . . *when* – stuff it all, fill my shoes with shit and call me Shirley! – in comes this guy with a sheet of paper in his mitt sporting a blob of red wax – the paper, not his mitt – and heads straight for Mr Greene. Debt-collector! Quick as a flash I shove aside the drab I'm chatting up and get between him and his quarry. 'Who are you?' he says, all poncey – grape up the bum type, you know. 'A friend,' I say. 'Balls,' he replies. 'No,' I riposte. '*Ball*, singular, premier appellation: *Cutting*. And not *your* friend. His!' Indicating Mr Greene in my rear, if you'll pardon the expression . . . Well, he stands his ground, the collector, I give him that. And I, of course, stand mine. In fact we stand eye to eye – yes and ball to ball – while all around there grows a deathly hush in the manner of such occasions. Very theatrical! [*Beat.*] And we wait – or rather I do – for him to escalate, feed me the line, give me the emotion. And he does, pricked on by a nervous laugh from the drab – quite a *bon palona*, as a matter of fact – I've left at the bar . . .

Him menacing: 'Do you mind shifting, friend?' Me, calm as a razor: 'As a matter of fact, sunshine, I do!' At which point I take out my little prodder here [*producing a dagger*] and rest it delicate-like just on the tip of his nose-hole, right here.

[*He demonstrates on his own nose.*]

He looks down, cross-eyed. [*Demonstrating*] Then back up at me. He says no more, his gob shivering shut.

'Now,' I say, 'I am well-known in these environs for a particular dislike I maintain for factors; or, as you may care to elevate your calling, debt-collectors. I hold them in no more worth than apple-squires or bawdy baskets. And when they come, such as your not-so-good-self, as bold as Brummagem, to harass and annoy, then it has been known for me to take this cuttle-bung of mine and perform a certain surgical operation from which my monicker derives. It is a simple operation but exceedingly effective . . .

[*He lets the dagger drop from his nose to his crotch, while with his other hand he gently cups his own testicles.*]

. . . requiring just two careful cuts . . .

[*He slips the tip of the dagger into the base of his scrotum.*]

One . . .

[*He mimes cutting and catching a testicle.*]

Two . . .

[*He mimes cutting and catching the other, then he slowly lifts his hand, holding it out to the audience. Pause. Then deliberately he closes his fist in a prolonged exquisite crushing gesture.*]

[*Pursing his lips*] Oooooo . . . . . !

[*Pause. He grins.*]

He passed out like a light. [*Beat.*] And when he came to, I made him eat the writ – paper, wax and all. [*Beat.*] Thus a debt was postponed and honour satisfied – all in one fell swoop . . . as we say in the theatre!

Going Home

Alma de Groen

Currency, Sydney 1977

Act 3

JIM:

There won't be any disappointment.
It's different now. I've changed!
How can I convince you?
[*Pause.*]
Look. I was happy this morning. Remember?
[*Pause.* JIM *stares at her.*]
You really don't believe me, do you?
Shit. What can I say to you? Listen. I went into the studio this morning and looked at my paintings – really looked at them – and they seemed wrong. Inadequate. And do you know something? I didn't care. Because I knew that it was a good feeling, because something had happened to me, I'd grown, and I'd be able to make the paintings grow with me, that eventually they'd catch me up, and then I'd outstrip them again, and then they'd catch me again.
[*Pause.*]
I've had the feeling many times, but this morning I realised something I'd never fully acknowledged before: that it'll go on all my life no matter where I am or what the circumstances are. It's a race that I hold with myself that only I can win or only I can lose. It doesn't matter where I run the race, as long as I run it and don't let anything stop me along the way.
[*Pause. He looks at* ZOE.]
I'm not going home because I failed here, or because I think it will be better. I'm going home simply because it's time now. I was born there and I want to live and work there. [*Gripping* ZOE*'s shoulders*] Do you believe me?
Come with me and you'll see.

My Name is Pablo Picasso

Mary Gage   Currency, Sydney 1984

PICASSO:

Idiots! Keep that arm up! Complete idiots! Did you hear them? When I think those cretins are the whole reason I came to Paris! I thought I'd find people who understood painting! Hah! It makes me laugh!

[*He laughs, loud, angry, bitterly.*]

Did you hear how Matisse laughed – in my face!

[*Imitating Matisse's laugh*] 'I'll show you!' he said. 'I'll make you beg for mercy! D'you call that a painting?' [*Pointing to* Les Demoiselles] 'You've made the modern movement ridiculous!' Hah! All he showed me was how stupid he is! What an idiot! So eager to please! Exhibiting before the paint's even dry! Explaining himself to fools! He's trotted out like a monkey on a stick at those terrible Steins' dinner parties . . . Hah! I'm glad Leo hated my painting! What a kiss of death if he'd liked it! D'you know he actually varnished the one you bought? To make it look better! People like that should buy picture postcards. They're not interested in art. All they're interested in is other idiots saying 'Aren't the Steins marvellous! You know, Matisse dines with them! How well they understand the modern movement.' Bah! Let them rot in Hell for all I care! I'm so happy to be rid of the whole phony, posing lot of them, I feel like laughing!

[*He does his Matisse laugh again.*]

Keep still! I haven't finished. And as for Braque! Did you see that silly fool sniffing round my painting? I thought he was going to lift his leg against it. Why did I waste my breath on him? I thought Braque at least had some sense. So I actually tried to explain. I said, 'Can't you see that this is the same as everything I have ever painted before? The one difference is, I'm not saying it prettily any more. Life is ugly. Life is sick. Life is short. You don't say that prettily. You say it like THAT!'

[*He slams his hand down on the table.*]

And what did Braque say at the end of all my talk? 'You might as well force me to eat rope and drink paraffin.'

[*He spits on the floor.*]

I should have saved my breath and shot him . . .

I haven't finished.

A Manual of Trench Warfare

Clem Gorman

Currency, Sydney 1979

Scene 6

MOON:

You think I can't look after myself, mate? Let me tell you, let me tell you a few things that happened after the boat and before you came into this trench. I was in the second wave onto that beach, Anzac Cove. Those blokes you mentioned, the ones that I was playin' cards with on the deck, well all of them died on the way to the beach or the way up the beach into the hills. I got to the top of the beach and when I flung meself down the bodies were so thick I couldn't touch the sand. There was blokes round me, some dying', some not, and they was jokin' among themselves like schoolboys which one of them would get to the next line of wire first. I saw three of them shake hands on a bet, get to their feet, and all three o' them was killed before they'd gone ten feet. I was on me own, that was the difference, that was what made me different, mate, I was on me own, I didn't make no bets, I kept me head on the job. I made it to the next fence, and I cut through it too. There musta been twenty Turks shootin' at me, that's what it felt like. I felt like paintin' a bullseye on me chest but I was in a bit of a hurry ter get somewhere. I moved forward

97

like that, with all me mates gone, hardly sleepin', not eatin', drinkin' water once every few hours, without a break, among men I didn't know, for three fuckin' days. I emptied me rifle more times than I've emptied me bum. I never saw a Turk, just me own kind dyin'. I got through. I didn't get a fuckin' scratch. I hardly had any contact with officers, they was mostly fightin' what you call a long range war from behind somewhere. So I just took it step by step, makin' me own decisions about when to move and when ter stay put. I dug this fuckin' trench, with two other blokes, and the front line was just up there; and it's still just up there, and before you came into this trench, me and various others had beaten back four major Turkish attacks. All the blokes who fought with me are dead, but I'm still 'ere. Because I know how ter look after meself. And I don't need no protectin'! I'm the one who's still here, all those other blokes, they're dead. They're all *dead*! You can't help me, Paddy. I'm smarter than you think, and tougher, too.

Away

Michael Gow

Currency, Sydney 1992

Act 4 Scene 2

TOM:

Yeah, that's what I had. An infection. Everyone knew I had some infection. I was sick. I was told the infection was running its course. That I had to fight. I did. One day a doctor came and sat on my bed and had a long talk with me. He told me that before I got completely well again I would get a lot worse, get really, really sick. And no matter how sick I got not to worry because it meant that soon I'd start to get well again. He was full of shit. He couldn't look me in the face to say it. He stared at the cabinet next to the bed the whole time. And the nurses were really happy whenever they were near me, but when I stared them in the face, in the end they'd look away and bite their lips. When I was able to go home the doctor took me into his office and we had another talk. I had to look after myself. No strain, no dangerous activity. Keep my spirits up. Then he went very quiet, leant over the desk, practically whispering how if I knew a girl it'd be good for me to do it, to try it. 'It', he kept calling it. It, it. I put him on the spot. What? Name it. Give it a name. He cleared his throat. 'Sexual intercourse'. But if I was worried about going all the way I could experiment with mutual masturbation. Know what that is?

I nearly spat in his face. You shocked?

So how about it? Help me. I'm going to get sick again. And I won't get better. Your parents won't find out.

Mine don't know. That I know. They want me to think I'm going to be as right as rain. They mustn't find out I know. They mustn't even suspect, the poor bastards. And you won't fill them in.

Will you? . . .

Now . . . what do you say?

[*Silence.*]

I'm a real creep, aren't I?

[*Pause.*]

I could build myself up.

Yes. I could build myself up. Do a Charles Atlas course. Would that help?

I'll do it.

The Kid

Michael Gow Currency, Sydney 1983

Scene 6

ASPRO:

You hate me. That's it, you hate me. That's why you drag me around all those offices. They say: 'No, you've come to the wrong place, Park Street, eighteenth floor.' We walk there. You know that's difficult for me in my condition. We get there. The girl says: 'No, you're in the wrong place. Why did they send you here? Clarence Street, third floor.' We walk there, all the way, in the boiling heat in the middle of the day. We get there. The girl says: 'No, this is the Occupational Section. Liverpool Street, ninth floor.' We walk there. When we get there it's lunchtime. The girl we have to see isn't there. By now I can hardly stand up. We have to wait. We have to take this ticket from this stupid machine and wait for our number to come up. We sit and sit and sit and it's hot and everyone's smelly and sweaty from walking the same streets all the time. We sit and sit and sit and listen to the *Sound of Music* 'Bossa Nova.' There's some smart arse wants them to see him first 'cause he's really important 'cause he's been there before and someone told him he wouldn't have to wait. But you always have to wait when somebody owes you something. We sit there. We sit and sit. All these cripples and fuckwits like that Irishman from Caringbah. I felt sorry for him, but, he couldn't stop chucking for months. Nothing of him. You're lucky I didn't ask him home with us. Then you'd have been sorry. *At last* the girl comes back from lunch and the numbers start rolling. The girl puts her lippy on behind the counter where everyone can see her, just so we all know how important she is and how we're all in the palm of her hand. You have to wait and wait and wait. Your number gets closer and closer and it gets hotter and hotter. Then, *oh, boy*! Someone's given up in despair so your number's even closer. *Then. At last.* It's your turn. You go over to the counter. She's bored and hot.

Goes 'tsk-tsk-tsk.' Rolls her eyes. At the desk behind the counter another girl. Hot. Bored. Rolls her eyes. Sweat in her mo. Rolls her eyes. Some poor sick bugger pours his heart out over the phone. Begging. Pleading for scraps. She's important too. Works in an office. Has a desk and phone. Goes home in the train reading *Cosmo*. Has tea with Mum and Dad. Complains about all the awful people she sees all day. Boyfriend Greg. Works in the Valuer General's. Comes over. Watch *Prisoner*. He works his finger up her crack.

Oh, I know it all. It's all true. They don't care what they say in front of me. I'm too sick to worry about. They talk away. I listen. She asks questions. Fills in the form. Rolls her eyes. Puts her hair behind her ear like this. It keeps falling over her face. She keeps putting it behind her ear 'cause it makes her feel important and busy. She says: 'Have you lodged a previous claim?' and I say 'yes' and start to explain. She grinds teeth, rolls eyes. Looks at the girl at the desk. Says: 'Well it's being attended to', and I say I can't wait any more. I'm sick. I'm sick. I'm getting sicker and sicker. [*To* DONALD].

You, you touch me, you little fairy. I'll smash your face in.

1841

Michael Gow   Currency, Sydney 1988

Act 2 Scene 10

GREEN:

Look what I found.

[*He holds up a plaster death mask of a man.*]

Remember him? My first day on the job. Jesus Christ I was nervous. Three of them I had to do. Fucked it right up. Two went down. Didn't feel a thing. But this bloke. Didn't get the rope right. Broke when he took up the slack. Fell right through. Lay there for a second, started crying and moaning. We had to stand him on one of the other blokes' coffins while we put a new rope around him. Jesus Christ he was upset. Remember him? Sorry. Anglican wasn't he? You micks go better than Anglicans as a general rule. Suppose you're glad to get out of the place. No more priests! Unless you end up down below. Plenty of them down there eh?

[*The* PRIEST *goes.*]

Stand up son. Nice and straight. Just measure you. It's best to be sure, every time. Never want to repeat that fuck up. You wouldn't like that. Hold that a second.

[*He hands him the mask.*]

Scared. Don't be. This knot we use now, goes here at the back of your head. Soon as you hit, whack, blackness. Don't worry about me son, I'm pissed and that's nothing new. Got this mask out of the pile, we're packing. Got a new gaol, up in Darlinghurst. We move up there at the end of the week. Poor bloke, when he opened his eyes and knew he had to go through it all again. I copped shit I can tell you. I'll see you tomorrow.

[*Takes the mask and goes.*]

Europe

Michael Gow

Currency, Sydney 1987

Act 4

DOUGLAS:

Thinking about how lucky you are having two million years of blood-soaked history. Counting your ruined churches and bomb craters and flaky paintings and immigrant workers. You can't stand them either. You hate them: That's what I really despise about this place, this continent. You're so proud of your culture, your history, you love pointing to the bullet holes and the place where the mob scraped the plaster on the palace wall. Every fucking castle and palace and museum and gallery and square I've dragged myself around looking for the courage to face you, all they arouse in me, all it suggests to me is the billions of poor fucking victims on this globe that suffered and died so you could have this wonderful continent. All those bastards who woke up one morning and saw the white sails on the horizon and thought, 'This is it, this is the end; it had to come.' That's what all your history does for me: makes me think of them. And all the rubbish heaps you had to set up as far away as possible, godforsaken holes where you could dump all your shit, all the crap that was getting in your way while you paddled around in your two million years of historical blood, adding a bit more blood every few minutes. And you: you have the hide to look down on us, the fucking gall to look down on us: us, the victims, the rubbish. Makes me want to vomit. Shit, why didn't I fall in love with someone from Wilcannia? You know what? I'm glad I don't have any more history than what I've got. What we have got's bad enough, I wouldn't want as much as you. Who needs that? It'd be unbearable. I think myself lucky. Maybe we don't have a rich culture. Big relief. Maybe ours is poor but honest. I was walking back from the ticket counter this morning and I heard this voice say, 'Scuse me, joo know where there's a toilet?' I swear to God my heart beat faster. I was on her side. All the

103

sods who've been duped into thinking this place, Europe, was more important, dragging themselves around it, filling your pockets, keeping your standards of living up. I felt part of this . . . army. The army of the conned. That girl looking for a dunny in a European railway station, the men trying to steal an hour from their wives to slip into a strip show while the wives scour Europe for a decent cuppa. This girl called 'Rhonda' sitting with her friends in a restaurant, calling out 'Haven't you got any pies?', and laughing 'til she cried. The widows staggering around the abbeys and palaces of a country that doesn't want to know them any more. My grandmother's brothers, all buried in a field in Belgium. I'm with them, I'm in that army. All of them who've gone through hell so all of you can stay on top.

All Stops Out

Michael Gow   Currency, Sydney 1991

SAM:

Remember when you first said you hate school. I despise school. It just gets in the way. That book I was reading on the beach that day, that had nothing to do with school. It was a book by someone I read about in a book about the novel we're supposed to study. I hate the stuff we're supposed to read, there's so much to read that's better, more interesting, more exciting, I keep reading that. I have to force myself to read these books. Whenever we're supposed to read *Romeo and Juliet* that's when I want to read Jane Austen. When we're supposed to read Andrew Marvell I want to read Isaac Asimov. Have you read *Foundation and Empire*? It's great. Whenever we're supposed to read Keats I want to read *Jude the Obscure*. I love reading but I hate school. It's torture. But I have to do it. If only I was free to just read whatever I wanted, just get lost in books and writers and ideas. But you have to come back to the theme of *Romeo and Juliet* and character in the modern novel and compare and contrast Andrew Marvell and . . . and a two headed cow. I'm no good helping you. I'm a fraud Danny. I don't even want to do Law. God, what am I saying? I'm doing it for my mother. Everytime she looks in on me with my desk lamp on and all the books stacked around the desk, I can feel her wanting me to be a genius, to get 501 out of 500 and become the world's greatest lawyer. All I want to do is read a book about something that's not on the course. I'm a fraud.

What would be really great would be if they just said read fifty books and see fifty films and go to ten foreign countries and learn ten poems and join a rock group and come back in two years and we'll give you the Higher School Certificate.

But we're stuck with this stuff. Cram it in and forget it two days after the exam. Oh let me out of here. I need some air.

Hence, knave, avaunt thee outside to thy bike.

On Top of the World

Michael Gow   Currency, Sydney 1987

Act 2

MARCUS:

I wish I could just sit down and have a little talk about something really meaningless with you. I do, I do. You know what I wish I was? One of those people that stand outside courthouses when they take in some child murderer or molester. The ones that hurl abuse and threaten to kill them. I wish I was like that, so sure of everything, so convinced, I wish I had kids to go home to, watch TV with and listen to them talk about the horrors of deviates and addicts and criminals and then sit back and watch our favorite characters going through their routines as doctors and policemen and schoolteachers in the Depression and then watch a news flash about some strange part of the world where the poor bastards don't have the benefits we have. Oh I wish I was like that, I do. Then I could talk. I would talk and talk. But I'm sorry, I see it all and know it's nothing but lying. I just see right through it. I see a few people having a good time at the expense of billions of other people living in agony. I'd open my mouth to have a chat and straight away I'd see them, in misery . . . and us . . . sitting here in the sunshine . . . I see through it . . . to talk I'd have to want those things . . . and it's lying . . . and it's not worth having . . . I don't have anything to say.

Sex Diary of an Infidel

Michael Gurr
Currency, Sydney 1992

Scene 10

MARTIN:

Are you tired?

[*Beat*]

I've got my second wind.

Let's go out.

So do it and let's go out.

It can wait.

[*Pause*]

[MARTIN *reads the room service menu, the video list.*]

You can get Maxi-Burgers, fresh oysters, french fries large, french fries medium.

[*Beat*]

French fries small. Tacos. Side orders of bacon. It's like Los Angeles. What do Filipinos eat? Mini pizza. Pizza for two. Garlic bread. [*Beat*]. Omelette. Oh. Between the hours of six and nine only. Aussie-style steak. Meat pie. Meat pie with french fries. Meat pie with – [*Throws menu aside, reads video list*] Michele Pfiefer. Harrison Ford. William Hurt. Jack Nicholson. Debra Winger. Johnny Depp. Shirley MacLaine, Tom Hanks, Meryl Streep. [*Beat*] Hungry? [*Beat*] Stallone. Big Arnie.

[*Pause*]

I wonder what it's like to be an American. I've got some American blood somewhere, on my father's side, but it's years back, back before they were really Americans.

[*Beat*]

I mean, what must it be like? To have the whole world, to see the whole world as if it was your own? America, the capital city of the world. Venice for your Disneyland, Manila for your red-light district. I was in this small town in Italy once. Staying in a hotel that looked onto a square. At about three in the morning, I woke up to hear a group of Americans sitting on the church steps singing the theme song from *The Brady Bunch*. Incredibly loud. And people, Italians, were opening their windows and asking for quiet and these Americans – they were bewildered. It was like someone telling them to stop having a good time in a Fun Park.

Spiders

Ron Hamilton

Univ. of Qld Press, Brisbane 1970

BOY:

Here. Here in these boxes. Every spider has its own box, so it can think over what it's done. Think over what it's done before I put an end to its thinking. Because I have that power, I have that power now to put an end to its thinking. [*He holds up a box.*] This was the first spider I caught. [*Pause.*] This spider is my father. [*Pause.*] My spider-father with his spider-business-suit and his spider-business-brain and the filthy, stinking, web he tried to trap me in for years. Did trap me in for years until I fought and struggled and got free.

[*Pause.*]

I don't want to join the rowing team . . . Yes, I know it's your old school. I know your name is on the board. Yes, I know all this, but I don't want to row . . . No, nor cricket neither . . . No, none of them. I want to be left alone to write . . . Write what? Well, poetry if you must know . . . Well, to hell with what they call me. I want to be me. ME! An individual. A person. Not the son of one of the old boys. But me. ME! ME! . . .

. . . Yes, I want to write. I have so much I want to say, so much I want to do. But the job takes up too much of my time . . . Yes, yes, been in the family for years. You've told me before. So many times you've told me, I'm sick to death of hearing about it . . . I don't owe you a thing. Not a damn thing . . . You brought me

108

into this world. You gave me my life. Now let me live it my way. Let me be myself. Let me BE! [*Pause.*] Well, it didn't take you long to find where I was, did it? You thought you'd trap me again. You thought you'd catch me and take me back and destroy me in your web, but I was too smart for you. I caught *you*. [*Pause.*] My father.

And who have we here? In this box? Of course, this was the second of my spiders. My mother. My spider-mother. That dear, sweet, bitch: my mother. She's in there now. In this box. With her pink spider-hair. Set three times a week, darling. And her flashing spider-rings on her smooth as silk, soft as her brain, spider-fingers. Do you like it? Really? It's just a little thing actually, that Harry and I picked up when we were on the Continent last. And her laugh. That sterile, vacuous laugh that echoes the thoughts in that sterile vacuous head. Committees, fêtes, bazaars, parties, first nights. My, my, what a busy woman you must be! How do you find time to give yourself so generously to these charities? What we would do without you, I daren't think. Charity? Ha-ha. Lady, my mother; my sweet generous, I'll-sign-you-fill-in-the-amount, spider-mother, doesn't give, has never given, and will never give a damn whether some slant-eyed oriental has enough food in his guts or whether half this country's population has cancer, T.B., heart complaints, or is spastic, just as long as that insufferable photographer from that weekly paper didn't snap me with my mouth open. Horrid little man. Just waits to catch me talking and Phoof! There I am for the whole country to laugh at. I *never* photograph well when my mouth's open, now do I, Harry? [*Pause.*] My father. My mother.

[*Pause.*]

Have you ever seen a spider spinning a web?

It's like a dance. A slow, sinister dance. The spider drops, inch by inch, unravelling the strands behind him. Down. Up. Down. Up. Round. Across. Over. Back. In. Out. Round. Back. It's like a dance. A slow, unhurried dance. An overture. An overture to a ballet of the dying. Up. Down. Up. Down. Round. Across. Back. Up. In. Out. Round. Back.

Have you seen a fly, or a beetle or any insect caught in a web? The spider sits there on the side. Waiting. Waiting for the first one to come along and get caught. Sometimes it takes a while, but they come, they come. First one. Then another. And another. Where one goes, the others follow. They struggle for a while, and then they submit. Give in. Accept . . .

I've only been here a week and already I've caught over twenty-four spiders.

No Names, No Packdrill

Bob Herbert   Currency, Sydney 1980

Act 2

REBEL:

Well, my Ma an' Pa was almost all the time in a state of war an' us kids was out there in no man's land coppin' it from both sides.

. . . Didn't help matters much, my ol' man bein' a nut case.

Well, they never locked him up, . . . but he was nuts, all right. Not all the time . . . just . . . [*looking at the bottle*] especially when he was on this stuff. On the whisky . . .

[*Pause*]

What they was really fightin' about, Ah think, was bein' locked in the same cage together. Usually weekends they'd do their fightin', 'cause that's when he'd do his drinkin'. Ma'd start naggin' him with an awful mean tongue, an' he'd start sayin' her family was nothin' but a gang o' rustlers an' moonshiners, an' she'd come back with some pretty tellin' comments about his family, an' if he was losin' the argument, which he mostly did, he'd start bouncin' her off the walls of the kitchen an' us kids'd get whumped just for bein' there. Then he'd get quiet an' mean an' get his shotgun an' say he was gonna finish us all off then shoot hisself. All Ah wanted him to do was reverse the order.

He'd herd us into the bedroom, make us kneel down at the beds an' say our prayers. 'Now, kiss each other goodby,' he'd say. Then he'd say: 'close your eyes.' Ah can still hear the clicks as he cocked both barrels. Ah'd look out the corner of an eye an' those barrels'd be pointin' right at me. Ah'd think, this time he's gonna do it . . . But he never did. [*Chuckling*] Obviously, eh? Then he'd say he'd changed his mind – and he'd go down into his tool shed where he'd have a bottle hid from Ma. Then Ma'd put us to bed an' we wouldn't see him till morning, except once, Ah remember, the shotgun went off down in the shed, an' Ma kept sayin': 'Thank God! Thank God! He's killed hiself.' But – no such luck. He only shot a hole in the wall of the shed.

Ah guess Ah deserved my share of spankin', like any kid . . . but he couldn't do it like other fathers, you know, just his hand or his belt. No, he'd have to use his boots, or a goddam great lump of wood, or what he really liked was to bail me up in the barn an' lay into me with a rawhide whip. God, how Ah hated that son of a bitch. How Ah still hate him.

[*Pause*]

They don't know where Ah am. One day – Ah was fifteen, just turned fifteen – he came at me with that rawhide whip. Instead of standing there like a mouse waitin' for a snake, Ah ran. An' Ah kept on runnin' until Ah got to LA.

No Room For Dreamers

George Hutchinson   Currency, Sydney 1981

CHIDLEY:

Look at the stars . . . they're always beautiful, always new, always different. You should see them in the bush.

They're so much brighter there. I remember one time, up near Lake Torrens, I saw them, really saw them, for the first time – clear, brilliant, beautiful. I just stood looking up at them until my neck ached and then I sat down and leaned back against a rock and looked and I looked until, gradually, I became aware of space, of the distance, that immense void between us and them. The longer I looked the more the sense of it grew until I could almost feel its terrible dark coldness. It was like a great icy chasm . . . I stood up and I stretched my arm up, out, into it. And then a strange futile feeling came over me. I felt like nothing. I felt that no one, nothing, out there, knew or cared. No one.

Low

Daniel Keene

Unpublished

Scene 15

JAY:

I'm talkin' about years ago, right? My old man used to take me.
He used to take me everywhere. He would've taken me around
the fuckin' world if he'd had, you know, the necessary. He's gone
now . . . a long time ago. But yeah, he took me there, more than
once. It's all changed now, right? I haven't been there since I was
a kid. I remember the Ghost Train . . . that fuckin' Ghost Train,
it scared the shit out of me. I got off. No, listen, Talk about dark.
The old man wasn't with me. He had this . . . thing about, you
know, bein' confined . . . somethin' in the war, he never said.
So I got off, right . . . and I don't know where the fuck I am. The
train's been jerkin' around in the dark. I was sick almost. I'd
already been on the Roller Coaster, and the Scenic Railway . . .
all those rides. I'm about to lose my lunch . . . and all this shit
I'd eaten, so I dive off the thing. Stumblin' around, you know,
scared shitless. It just went on and on . . . and I could hear all
the other kids screamin', like in the distance, you know? I'm
walkin' into all this shit, all this stuff they got hangin' down . . .
spider webs, rubber hands . . . bones and skulls . . . and I go
crazy, right, I'm tearin' the place up . . . I'm tryin' to get out . . .
and then I hear these footsteps behind me, right, someone's
runnin' towards me . . . and I freak . . . it's pitch dark and
there's someone runnin' at me down this long black tunnel . . .
so I brace myself, and I'm waitin' and I hear this breathin', this
. . . panting . . . and it's gettin' closer . . . then it brushes past
me and I'm kickin' at it and screamin' and it's tryin' to hold me
down, it's got hold of me and I'm thrashin' around . . . and I
start gettin' dragged. I'm bein' dragged along the tracks . . . so
fuckin' dark I couldn't see my hand in front of my face. So
finally, with me fightin' all the way, we get to the end of the
tunnel, out into the light . . . and it's my old man's got a hold of

113

me . . . he's white as a sheet . . . fuckin' terrified . . . so terrified he couldn't speak . . . and there's blood streamin' down his face where I'd kicked at him in the dark. He'd raced in when he saw I wasn't on the train when it come out . . . he'd raced into the tunnel . . . scared shitless like he was of the dark, 'cause of the war or somethin' like that . . . he never fuckin' told me . . . and he's rescued me, right? I could feel him tremblin', you know . . . tremblin' like a . . . like a bird or somethin'.

[*Beat*]

Who's buyin' the next round?

Furtive Love

Peter Kenna

Currency, Sydney 1980

Act 2

TOM:

You're so hard on yourself. I first made love to another man the night before my wedding. Some of the chaps I worked with gave me a stag party. One of them had often made it clear he was fond of me but I'd never taken him seriously. I was in love with the girl I was going to marry. There was, of course, a lot of drink at the party but that wasn't what made this man seem suddenly attractive. For some reason – perhaps it had been inside me all the time and I wasn't aware of it – I dared to consider that another man *might* be attractive. And that was all it needed. I went home to his place, stayed the night with him and the next morning I got married. I discovered I was in love with two people who each satisfied a different need in me. But the man believed I'd let him down. After a while we began to quarrel. We'd make up, but it would always break out again: his distress at the situation. Eventually he killed himself. And I thought that I would die too – of grief and guilt. So I turned to the other person I loved. I told my wife everything. If I'd been sane enough to stop and think about it I might have realised she'd be appalled. But I wasn't. And she's never permitted me to make love to her since. Never even touched me with a gesture of concern. We have an arrangement because of the children. She won't divorce me if I behave discreetly. I don't want a divorce. I still love her. I'm not a fool, Joe. I suspect you all regard my caution as a joke. I'm aware I've probably become a rather boring person. But outside my bedroom, I'm never sure of how I *ought* to behave. And I walk in dread of another calamity.

You're so hard on yourself. It's life, Joe. It's love.

115

Foreskin's Lament

Greg McGee
Victoria Univ. Press, Wellington, 1989

Act 1

IRISH:

Jesus, do we have to? All this extra training isn't good for me. The fitter I get, the more effort it takes to get exhausted.

. . . And I haven't seen the sheila since Monday, I'll be getting wet dreams soon.

. . . It's so bloody boring. Push, pull your head out, run about till you find another heap of fellas, find a hole to stick your head in where it's dark, push again, pull it out, run along to the next heap. You won't believe this, but at home intelligent conversation at the bottom of a ruck was not unknown. Over here, no-one talks, all you hear is grunts, growls, belches, the odd fart, and occasional snapping noises which might be teeth clamping or bones breaking, I mean you wouldn't know, it's so bloody dark you wouldn't know you'd died till the bloody whistle blew. My idea of purgatory is doing endless ruck and runs with Tupper screaming encouragement.

. . . The only one here with the right attitude is Foreskin, he doesn't give a thruppenny stuff. He's got style, that lad. Did I tell you about last Saturday night after that do at Grubby's? There we were, caught red-handed, high as kites, right out of our chooks, going down a one-way street the wrong way. Next minute a siren goes, a police car pulls us over, and this traffic officer character walks up to us – big, fat fella he was. Well, Foreskin winds down his window blithe as you like, not a worry in the world, having stubbed out a roach he was drawing on not a second before. This officer fella leans down to the window and asks Foreskin, 'Did you not see the arrows, son?' 'Arrows, officer?' says Foreskin, 'I didn't even see the Indians!' Now, it may or may not be original, but that's timing, that's class.

Act 1

TUPPER:

I'm a worried man!

[*Silence. He stares up at the ceiling, then picks up the large boot off the table in front of him with the air of a man finally arrived at a solution.*]

Now, take a good long look at this!

[TUPPER *flourishes the boot, then dangles it by the laces in front of each player as he stalks about.*]

It's a boot, a big, heavy, dirty boot. Now, what's it for, eh? What's it for?

It is not for keeping your feet dry in the puddles. If it was, why's it got this hard bit at one end, eh? No, no, no, no, no! It's hard at one end so you can kick things and not hurt your big toe.

Like the ball . . . certainly the ball, certainly the ball. But if, on occasion the ball has got the odd bit of hair on it, or an ear or such-like, then we'll give it the benefit of the doubt and kick shit out of it first and let the ref ask questions after. Don't be too obvious, mind, we're grown men and we know the game – a bit of ruthlessness, a bit of hate. I know most of those lads and I'm telling you a bit of the old boot in the right place at the right time and they'll throw it in. We've got to be absolutely uncompromising, sicken them in the first twenty minutes so that they don't want to play. Kick and rake anything within yards of the ball, they'll lose their appetite pretty damn quickly. This is . . . psychological.

. . . Stands to reason. Doesn't matter how brave they are, how badly they want to win, when they've had it in the swede at one ruck, they're going to be just that much slower getting to the next one.

Now, Clean, Mean, you boys are the key here. I'm not going to say too much to you individually at this point because we're still two days away from the game and I wouldn't expect you to keep it in your heads that long. But listen, Clean, I've been more impressed with you lately, much more ruthless. I don't know whether it was that kick in the head or joining the force that did it, but keep it up son.

[TUPPER *pats* CLEAN *on the head appreciatively.*]

Mean, you've got to show some improvement son. I'm telling you this for your own good – if you want to make the rep team this year, you'll have to get that edge. Last week I saw you step over some bod on the ground on the way to a ruck – the ref was on the other side – blind! Son, a true rep player would not have stepped over that bastard.

[TUPPER *grabs a handful of* MEAN's *hair and shakes* MEAN's *head.*]

He'd have stepped on him, run through him! You're the prime example of someone who's got to get a little more hate into his game otherwise the glories of the rep stuff will be little more than a dream.

Now Irish – Jeez, you'd be a mis-shapen looking bastard – idea! Now, where I come from, a No. 8 is not an imitation loosie, all right? I want you to stay in the tight all day. I want you to be like those pit ponies, blind from lack of light – and not for any other reason mind. However, you will be playing off the end of the lineout. For two reasons: (a) you're as fast as my grand-mother downing Guinness on payday, and secondly, you're as ugly as sin. I want you to go off the end of that lineout like a rocket, straight at their first-five. Now, I'm not expecting you to catch him every time, but if you can get within a couple of yards of him, he'll get a good look at your ugly mug and if he's got any brains at all, he'll be scared shitless for the rest of the game and drop the ball. That's the key, ball on the ground, we know what to do with it.

Righto! So that's the general strategy! We kick shit out of everything above grass height, and we keep the ball ahead of us. I know you forwards will do me proud.

I've Come About the Assassination

Tony Morphett Univ. of Qld Press, Brisbane 1970

YOUNG MAN:

Violent? Violent, are we? Tell me what else we've ever been shown Dad. Eh Dad? Eh? What else have we even seen, eh? Teenager ordered the bomb dropped on Hiroshima, eh Dad? Bit of a kid worked out the answer to the Jewish problem, eh Dad? All you kids. All so violent. You were a violent kid, Dad, weren't you? Fighting in the revolution. Cutting people's throats and all. Who was it told you to cut the throats, Dad? Teenager was it? Or was it some old bastard with a grey moustache and one foot in the grave? Eh, Dad? Eh? Who nutted out the area bombing on Germany? Who worked out the flying bombs for England? Who said for every one bomb that drops on our kids, we'll drop ten on theirs? Rotten pimply faced teenage hooligans, wasn't it? Eh, Dad? You know why you say we're violent? Because some of us have taken a wake up to you. I wouldn't swat a fly for you or anyone else your age. But if I needed to, for myself, I'd cut God's throat. I'm not killing for old men in parliaments. I'm killing for myself. And do you know why, Dad? Because all along, right down the line from the man with the club killing on the witch doctor's say-so, right through to the poor helpless bastards spitted on bayonets in what a warm, fat bishsop could call a just war, right down the line, there's always been another generation of kids to send off to get killed. But this is it. Since that bomb. If we muff it, it . . . is . . . this . . . generation . . . that . . . picks . . . up . . . the . . . cheque. So that's why I'm not listening to anyone but me. And I'm not killing for anyone but me. And for all sorts of confused reasons, I am going to kill that man in the car. If the light is good, and the gas man doesn't come.

119

Sunrise

Louis Nowra

Currency, Sydney 1983

Act 2

CLARRIE:

What would you know, a mind grubby with a hunger for power. You have no idea how magnificent it was.

A white light so intense you felt like a blind man first seeing the sun. Or the dawn of creation. Majestic, god-like, terrifying.

The beauty of it, the horror of it, so overawed me that, as I was driving back from the blast site, I got lost. After a while I came upon what looked like black melons scattered on the sand. When I was closer I saw that they were Aboriginals buried up to their necks, afraid of the black greasy smoke heading their way. 'The devil spirit' they called it. The old men of the tribe were standing in front of the group, pathetically trying to scare it away with their woomeras but they couldn't compete with white fellas' magic. All those Aboriginals are now blind. For days I was unable to sleep because my brain was soaked with this frightening, beautiful vision. It had come into being because men had imagined it. We wanted it! We had made it real! We were now capable of making real anything we imagined; truly, a dangerous age to be in. Men are barbarians with the creative gifts of gods.

[*Pause.*]

I was young and idealistic. Only idealists could have developed the atomic bomb. Only young, extraordinary scientists would have been arrogant enough to have wanted to perfect something so terrible in its power and yet so exquisite in its obedience to natural laws. It isn't old people who are going to destroy us, it's the young because they're never aware of the consequences of anything they do . . .

Being a politician, don't you feel responsible for politicians killing more than one hundred million people this century? Once I was consumed, like you, by certainties, now I am

120

possessed by doubts. I don't like you, Richard, you're a child in long pants. You believe everything you say; you're a dangerous man . . .

Jesus, I hate this era, this era where people see their lives and the lives of others through ideologies and politics. There is no such thing as the State; there is only hunger, imagination, pain, pleasure, love and friendship . . .

Cosi

Louis Nowra   Currency, Sydney 1992

DOUG:

It was the fault of the psychiatrist. I'd been seeing him because of my pyromania – that's a person who likes lighting fires – but you probably know that being university educated – but you know the problem with pyromania? It's the only crime where you have to be at the scene of it to make it a perfect crime, to give yourself full satisfaction. 'Course, that means the chances of you getting caught are greater, especially if you're standing in front of the fire, face full of ecstasy and with a gigantic hard on. So, the cops got me and I'm sent to a shrink. He tells me that I've got an unresolved problem with my mother. I think, hello, he's not going to tell me to do something Oedipal, like fuck her or something . . . but that wasn't the problem. My ego had taken a severe battering from her. He said I had better resolve it, stop her treating me like I was still a child. It made some sort of cosmic sense. I had to stand up to her. So I thought about it and realised I had to treat it like a boxing match, get the first punch in, so to speak, to give me the upper hand in our relationship. She had five cats. One night I rounded them up, put them in a cage, doused them with petrol and put a match to them. Then I opened the cage door and let them loose. Well, boy, oh, boy, what a racket! They were running around the backyard burning and howling – there's no such thing as grace under pressure for a burning cat, let me tell you. I hid in the shrubs when mum came outside to see what was happening. Totally freaked out, she did. Five of them, running around the backyard like mobile bonfires. I figured I'd wait a couple of hours til the cats were dead and mum was feeling a bit sorry for herself and I'd knock on the front door and say to her 'Hi, mum, I've come to talk about our unresolved conflicts' but, oh, no, one of those cats ran into the house. In a couple of minutes the whole bloody house was alight and within half an hour there was no bloody front door to knock on. [*A beat.*] If it wasn't for that damn cat, I wouldn't be in here.

The Golden Age

Louis Nowra   Currency, Sydney 1989

Act 1 Scene 8

FRANCIS:

Are you looking at the sunset?

[*Startled,* BETSHEB *turns around.*]

[*Smiling*] I'm not a monster . . . no more running.

[*Silence. He walks closer to the river.*]

Look at us reflected in the water, see? Upside-down.

[*He smiles and she smiles back. Silence.*]

So quiet. I'm not used to such silence. I'm a city boy, born and bred. You've never seen a city or town, have you? Where I live there are dozens of factories: shoe factories, some that make gaskets, hydraulic machines, clothing. My mother works in a shoe factory. [*Pointing to his boots*] These came from my mother's factory.

[*Silence.*]

These sunsets here, I've never seen the likes of them. A bit of muddy orange light in the distance, behind the chimneys, is generally all I get to see.

[*Pause.*]

You'd like the trams, especially at night. They rattle and squeak, like ghosts rattling their chains, and every so often the conducting rod hits a terminus and there is a brilliant spark of electricity, like an axe striking a rock. 'Spisss!' On Saturday afternoon thousands of people go and watch the football. A huge oval of grass. [*Miming a football*] A ball like this. Someone hand passes it, 'whish', straight to me. I duck one lumbering giant, spin around a nifty dwarf of a rover, then I catch sight of the goals. I boot a seventy-yard drop kick straight through the centre. The crowd goes wild!

[*He cheers wildly.* BETSHEB *laughs at his actions. He is pleased to have made her laugh.*]

Not as good as your play.

[*Pause.*]

This is your home. My home is across the water, Bass Strait.

[*Silence.* STEF *rolls over and ends up near* FRANCIS' *feet.*]

What is it about you people? Why are you like you are?

[BETSHEB *gathers up her flowers. As she stands she drops a few.*]

Don't go.

[*He picks up the fallen flowers.*]

I was watching you pick these. My mother steals flowers from her neighbour's front garden so every morning she can have fresh flowers in her vase for Saint Teresa's portrait. She was a woman centuries ago. God fired a burning arrow of love into her. [*Smiling*] When it penetrated here, Saint Teresa could smell the burning flesh of her heart.

123

The Watchtower

Louis Nowra Unpublished

ANDREW:

They come at first, every weekend, then the period stretches into a year, and they come every second weekend. By the third, every two months, by the fourth, every six months or when they remember. It's understandable, I mean when will we be cured? What is there to talk about? [*Parodying*] I had a wonderful week, I took my temperature, I spat a lot, coughed all night, spot of blood here, there. Read. Talked. Talked about what? Oh, what we always talk about. Told the same jokes. What do Attila the Hun and Winnie the Pooh have in common? The 'the' [*She smiles*] You think it's funny?

Well, you are from Queensland.

I have an Uncle who occasionally visits. He stands over there and shouts to me. [*Demonstrating vocally*] 'How are you, Young Andy?' [BEATRICE *laughs. He smiles in response to her laughter*]

I've been here six years; since I was sixteen.

I was coughing at school. My mother took me to the doctors. He was quick to diagnose what I had. My mother went white and said nothing. The next day we were having dinner. My father, my sisters, my mother, and as I was eating, I noticed a curious thing. I was putting a piece of meat to my mouth and realised my fork wasn't as shiny as everyone else's. I had been given the old cutlery. Then I noticed that my plate was different from everyone else's. I said nothing and later on noticed that my towel was alone on a rack, my bedclothes soaked with disinfectant and whenever my family talked to me they stood further away and there was one more thing; they were always looking at me, pretending not to, fear in their eyes, real fear, waiting for me to pass it on to them. Not fear that I would die, but fear they would catch it. It. *It.* Always it. Never it's real name. It got worse; so I came here. Away from them, away from contaminating them with *It*. So it's good that they don't come up. They would stand so far away I'd need binoculars to see them.

ANDREW:

Australia's at war.

If I can't stay here and be with you, then I'd like to fight for something other than myself.

[*A beat*]

I want to DO something.

[*A beat*] In Europe they don't see some of the stars we see here at the bottom of the world.

[*A beat*]

If I don't fight, then there is no future. You're waiting to be cured. If I'm down in Sydney, that's all they'll be doing – waiting. Like hibernation. If I join up I have a cause. A sense that I am not waiting, but doing something for a cause other than myself. I'll fight with a sense that I have a future, that I will have earnt us being together, rather than sitting here in this garden, the world far away. [*Pause*] When it is day there, it'll be night here. When you're awake, I'll be asleep. I'll be dreaming of you, while you're sitting here, and when I'm thinking of you, you'll be dreaming of me. Like some invisible cord bringing day and night together, dreaming and thinking together.

[*He laughs*]

You know what love is? The right to say stupid things.

I get so frustrated. I touch you like this and I can't believe how powerful my feelings for you are – like an electric current and I can't breathe. The touch of your skin. [*Putting fingers on her lips*] I touch your lips. I touch your lips. And I . . .

[*Grabbing her*] Beatrice.

[*He kissses her passionately before she can react*]

[*He steps away*]

[*Pause*]

That's the first time I've kissed you on the lips. I'm not dead. I won't die from it. And anyway, I don't care if I did.

125

I know it's a risk. But I want to take it. Even if it meant infecting me. I want to be as close to you as possible; just once. You won't harm me. I couldn't be on the other side of the world thinking I had never kissed you, never made love to you. If I don't take a chance, if you don't, then our love isn't worth it. All or nothing in these times.

[*Pause*]

You won't hurt me.

Here. We'll make love here. So the whole of Sydney can see.

Confessions from the Male

Murray Oliver   Currency, Sydney 1984

Scene 7

HUSBAND:

[*letter in hand*] Well, she's left me, the bitch. Writ me a note an' left me. I'll read it to youse. [*Opening out the letter*] 'Dear Phillip' – now don't get up, I'm not connected to royalty.

[*He pauses, then continues reading.*]

'Dear Phillip, I have left'. [*To the audience*] Bloody obvious, isn't it! I come in lookin' for me tea and she's not here; of course she's left, and gotta write me a bloody novel about it . . . [*Reading on, focussing unsteadily on the letter*] 'Cannot stand it any more. I have no time to myself.' Signed, 'Elizabeth the Slave'.

[*Pause.*]

What a load of crap! What a load of rubbish! Now, I'm a reasonable sort of a bloke. You just have a look at what she's gotta do around here. Bugger all!

[*Pause.*]

All she's gotta do is get up in the morning when I get up and make me breakfast; now I don't eat much for breakfast, you know – coupla eggs, coupla tomatoes, sausage or two, and a bit of steak to go with it, coupla pieces of toast, bit of Vegemite and some cornflakes.

[*He pauses, rocking.*]

Well, of course you don't put the bloody Vegemite on the cornflakes! Then all she's gotta do is push me out the door and I'm off to work, out of her hair for the rest of the day. She's just gotta wake up the kids shove some breakfast in their faces, make 'em a sandwich, throw 'em in the car, throw the kids in the car and drive 'em off to school – she's back home by half-past eight. That's not much to do, you know. Simple! Then she can come home, sit down, and have a rest.

[*Pause.*]

I'm a reasonable sort of a bloke. 'Course she'd realise she's gotta wash the breakfast dishes. While she's about it, she might as well wash the clothes, then she could wash the windows, wash the floor, and while she's still got her hands wet she could run out the front and wash the porch – that's 'porch' not 'Porsche', we don't have a Porsche – then she could come inside and do a bit of vacuuming, a bit of vacuuming never hurt anyone, she could vacuum the lounge, vacuum the hall, she could sweep the kitchen, sweep the bathroom, give the bath a quick rinse, and do the dunny while she's about it, make up the beds, make up a shopping list, and toddle off to work.

[*Pause.*]

She's got a bludge of a job, you know, doesn't start till ten o'clock, back home by half-past three, pick up the kids on the way, make 'em a peanut-butter sandwich, out to play. Then she can put on the tea. Beef Stroganoff, Boulliaboisse a la Richleau – something nice and simple. Then she could whip outside and get a breath of fresh air; while she's out there she might as well mow the lawn – someone's gotta do it – and then,
Rake the leaves,
Sweep the drive,
Wash the car,
Cut the edges,
Trim the hedges,

Burn the rubbish,
Burn the cat,
Burn the bloody house, for all I care!
[*Pause.*]
I dunno why she left. I'm a reasonable sort of bloke.
She musta been bored. Musta been.

Scene 17

JIM:

Righto. This is the part of the show that you've all been waiting for. This is where I get to confess. Well, I don't want to disappoint any of you, but I've got nothing to confess. There's nothing wrong with me. I'm okay . . . Okay . . . [*Arms folded, and a bit shuffly on his fee, fidgety almost*] Okay.
[*Pause.*]
Well, I haven't always danced around on my feet like this. I call it prowlin' around like a tiger.
[*He laughs it off.*]
And I haven't always put my hands under me muscles like this, to make 'em look a bit bigger, and pushed me shoulders forward . . . I've done all that since I've been about twelve or thirteen. I don't want the other guys to think I'm a bit weak or anything, and besides, the girls like that sort of image, don't they? Some of the other guys said they did. I dunno.
[*He's becoming a bit nervous now, getting out of his depth.*]
Well, I –
[*He bumps backwards into the table.*]
I didn't notice that table there before. Musta been there, eh? Well, my voice isn't normally like this. I've put that on since I was about twelve or thirteen too. I don't want anyone to think I might be immature or anything . . .
[*He's getting a bit more nervy.*]
My normal voice is a little bit softer [*lowering his voice*] . . . about here . . . actually it's a bit lower than that [*lowering his voice further*] about here . . .

[*Pause.*]

I suppose I should talk to other guys, and to girls too, about why we all put on a big front – you know, a big image – and we're all too scarred to show any cracks in the mirror . . . [*shuffling nervously*] I wrote a bit of a poem about all this [*very embarrassed*] but youse already think I'm a bit of a dag. I might reead it to you later.

Yeah.

[*He turns and wipes his hand across his brow.*]

The Last of the Knucklemen

John Powers   Penguin, Melbourne 1974

TARZAN:

All right. Now let me put the lot of you straight. Number one: assault on anyone, for any reasosn, during a shift of works warrants instant dismissal. No exceptions. No 'ifs' or 'buts'. Out! On the spot. And if it'd happened while I was there, fat man, your feet wouldn't have touched the ground. Number two: if there'd been any of this bullshit about all for one and one for all, the rest of youse'd be booted down the road right after him. Quick-smart! This isn't General Motors. And it ain't B.H.P. You're day labourers on a wildcat mine, paid by the hour to jump when you're told to jump, and run when you're told to run. You're not hired to be smart-alecs and talk-back merchants. Get that into your dumb skulls. None of this bullshit about 'rights'. You can stay, or you can go. That's it. And if they're not enough 'rights' get the fuck off before I bounce you off. But don't stay on my crew and bitch about not liking the way you're told to do your work. All right? [*Faces them defiantly*]

Number three: this little turn you've stacked on has put my

job on the line. I'm paid to sort youse bastards out. And a blow-up when I'm off the site's worse than one I'm here to handle. I'm gonna have some answering to do. I'm gonna be under pressure to roll some heads. So saying I'm not too bloody pleased about it's the understatement of the century. My arse's stickin' right out that window because of youse bastards!

. . . You're my crew, and you've walked off the job. Time's been lost. And nothing in this game's as precious as time. Not even God.

You've pushed your luck as far as it'll go, fat man!
I decide the rights around here, mate! And I'm tellin' you you've got no right to thump an engineer – no matter what he calls you. Yell for me. Let me know what he said. And I'll sort the prick out. Me! Nobody else.

. . .

If you're wanting me to go right through you, mate, you're doing everything just perfect!

You're on my crew! And if you don't like that, get the hell out. Right now. But if you stay, and step outta line one more time, I'll slam your head right up your arsehole.

[*Straightens up, staring at Pansy with hatred. The impression is that if Pansy makes the slightest move Tarzan will spring at him. After a moment he turns to the others*]

Now let's get one last thing straight. There'll be no more walk-offs on this job. And if anyone as much as suggests it, I'll have his balls for it. Savvy? I'm not asking you to fall in love with your work. You're here because it suits you. Nobody asks you any awkward questions. Nobody tries to find out what the hell you're running from. And as soon as you don't need to be here any more you can bugger off. But not me. I'm here to stay. This's my turf. And I don't play games about anything that's likely to get me bounced off it. So be told!

Now I'm gonna sort this mess out. And I'm gonna be saying we'll be out there tomorrow morning for a day's work – same as any other day. And all this shit's gonna be behind us. Right?

[*Waits till he sees the heads nodding*]
All right.

Popular Mechanicals

Keith Robinson, William Shakespeare, and Tony Taylor

Currency, Sydney 1992

Act 2 Scene 1

SNUG:

A funny thing happened to me on the way to the theatre this evening. Anyhow. What did Ethelred the Unready say when he saw the mammoths coming over the hill? I'm not ready! What's the difference between a well dressed man and a sabre toothed tiger! A well dressed man wears a doublet and hose and a sabre toothed tiger just pants. [*Pant pant pant.*] What did William the Conqueror and Alexander the Great have in common? They were both big worriers. Warriors. What did Alfred the Great and Simon the Pieman have in common? The. How do you fit four mastodons onto a pony? Two in front and two in the back. Speaking of ponies, I was going to buy a carthorse the other day, and the man said 'come in', he said – so I went inside the stable and there was a horse lying on the floor with a lotta blankets and sheets covering him up, he said 'that horse'll cost you some money', I said 'it's dead isn't it', he said 'no', I said 'how much do you want for it' he said 'a pound', I said 'a pound', I said 'Blimey, he hasn't got any shoes on', he said 'Well, he's not up yet.'

So, eventually I got the horse outside and I tried to get on and every time I tried to get on he started to kick and he kicked so hard he got his foot in the stirrups, dropped his foot right in the stirrups, I said 'Well', I said 'if you're going to get on I'm going to get off!'

So, I got on the horse and it fell down, so I picked it up 'cos I'm a hefty lad you see, well I got on again and it fell down again, and I told the man I was down. I said 'this horse is no good to me, every time I get on he falls down, and haven't you got some nice horses there, you've got eight or nine in a string,' I said 'I'll have the one in the middle,' he said 'Don't take the one in the middle, they'll all fall down.'

131

I've just come back from the May Day revels, always have a wonderful time at the May Day revels, because I haven't got one of those wives who says where've you been, how much have you spent, who've you been with, she doesn't say that. No, she comes with me!

I'd like to do a few impressions if I may. Sir Thomas More. [*Adjusts hat.*] Thou dirty rat. Sir Walter Raleigh. [*Adjusts hat.*] Judith, Judith, Judith. Isabella of Spain. [*Adjusts hat.*] I vant to be alone. So like a man. Robin Hood [*Adjusts hat.*] If I know the Sheriff of Nottingham he'll stick to the ridges. Well, how dost thou know what they sounded like?

Hate

Stephen Sewell

Currency, Sydney 1988

Scene 7

MICHAEL:

You fathered us, raised us; set out our choices and chose for us; you made us run the maze of your mind till we thought we were you and then you spat us out like phlegm to infect the world; you crippled us! I sat here, Father, in this empty chapel; empty every day of the year, the doors locked, sat here in the dust to escape you; sat here in the corner to play marbles on these stones while the storm of your life battered at the walls outside. That was peace for me: an empty room in a dead religion; did you choose that for me, also? Who's real! You or me? Which one of us is the fake? I don't want it! I loved you, Father, loved you till the teeth of your love began to rip my insides out; till my soul crawled with insects, I loved you; and then I hated you more than I thought anyone could hate another. You can't have her! Is that what we are? Your fury given form? You broke and shaped each one of us: Raymond, your treachery and deviousness; Celia your

132

willpower – What am I? Your fool? I am your fool; played fool to your schemes and dramas; watched from the sidelines, found safety in the cracks of your armour; let myself be fooled, hid myself; thought life could be lived across the thin stretch of a smile – Who speaks now? You or me? Am I your fool, Father? The end of all your dreams; this product, me? Then look at yourself! We come now, Father. You called us here; now review your work. Your carving's done, your creations complete. I won't let you! Celia! Take anyone but her! You made love impossible, but love remains. There is love here, Father; love amongst the diseased; love that comes from another's courage in pain; I love her! Father, forgive me! Stop! We're here, Father; your children! We're here!

The Father We Loved on a Beach by the Sea

Stephen Sewell   Currency, Sydney 1980

Scene 12

DAN:

I used to be frightened – of getting arrested, you know. There's no time any more. It sort of curls up and dies inside you. After a while you can't feel yourself. You do something and five minutes later you can't remember what. It's like being lowered into eternity where everything happens at once but nothing changes. Time embraces you and then one night leaves you in some sordid hotel room wondering what your name is and how come you didn't drive a truck. Your hands shake – you can't light a match or something like that. You don't eat because you haven't got the time, and then you begin to forget to eat. You sleep in your clothes, you begin to smell, your skin turns grey.

You watch it all with a mild sense of curiosity and distaste. Healthy, vibrant people enjoying themselves look like monsters. You can't stand to talk to people. And slowly the things that caused you to join the struggle – the compassion, the outrage at injustice – die, and you become a much more ugly and diseased thing. That's what happened to Gris. The cops didn't kill him. They can hang up his body till it turns green, he'd already crawled out of it and climbed into the chants and the songs and the posters. Did you see 'em? The day they got him the streets were plastered: 'We are with you, Ramon Gris!' I saw him a week ago – a revolutionary's got nothing. No family, no friends, no children or lovers. You kill them inside you so they can't be hurt or hurt the revolution. The revolution, comrade. Not the Vietenamese revolution, not the Irian Jaya revolution, but The Revolution. It sure is funny comin' back to nothin', ain't it, Danny boy? You fuckin' said it, buddy. Sure is fuckin' funny. Haw fuckin' haw.

Dreams in an Empty City

Stephen Sewell   Currency, Sydney 1986

Scene 10

WILSON:

I have no need of your pity! You think you know the world. Let me show you the world. Look around you, Chris. What do you see? Tables? Chairs? Concrete? Glass? No; power. None of this is real, what's real is power: power put it here, power can take it away. It can erect buildings and throw them down, create lives and tear them apart. What are human beings compared to it? Lives are spent acquiring it, hoarding it, disbursing it; every lust and passion human beings are capable of is animated by it. It's more sought after than gold; men debase themselves for it, murder for it. Power, Chris, empty power. Is there anything more contemptible than man?

Man has damned himself!

Let me show you what I know!

[*He begins to pull the curtain aside.*]

Let me show you the power of evil! The city, Chris; one of the most beautiful cities in the world. A city sprung from greed and ambition, built from human flesh, every building the grave of a labourer whose life was less important than the profit its construction meant. The city, Chris, thrown up by finance and speculation, conceived in bribery, corruption and murder. A sparkling, empty edifice of dreams and nightmares. Listen to it, Chris, listen to it sigh; listen to its misery, its glory, its hunger. Feel the hum as power flows through it, organising it, animating it, connecting every part of it from the magnate in his penthouse to the single mother in her room. The city, Chris, the city of death glistening in the light of its own conceit. All this could be yours, nothing stands in your way. Know what men are and the world is yours. Stand here and imagine yourself the ruler of what you see, feel its power inside you and tell me honenstly there's anything outside it, anything more real. This is what I know! This is the horror of our life!

The One Day of the Year

Alan Seymour Angus & Robertson, Sydney 1977

Act 2

HUGHIE:

Why couldn't you leave them alone? Those two poor old boys having their quiet talk? Does everyone have to be as rotten as you are before you can enjoy Anzac Day?

. . . Do you know what you're celebrating today? Do *you*? Do you even know what it all meant? Have you ever bothered to dig a bit, find out what really happened back there, what this day meant?

Oh, Wacka - what would he know about it?

What does the man who was there ever know about anything? All he knows is what he saw, one man's view from a trench. It's the people who come after, who can study it all, see the whole thing for what it was –

Wacka was an ordinary soldier who did what he was told. He and his mates became a legend, all right, they've had to live up to it. Every year on the great day they've had to do the right thing, make the right speeches, talk of the dead they left there. But did any of them ever sit down and look back at that damn stupid climb up those rocks to see what it meant?. . .

How do I *know*? Didn't you shove it down my throat? [*He has plunged over to bookcase against wall, drags out large book.*] It's here. Encyclopaedia for Australian kids. You gave it to me yourself. Used to make me read the Anzac chapter every year. Well, I read it. The official history, all very glowing and patriotic. I read it . . . enough times to start seeing through it. Do you know what that Gallipoli campaign meant? Bugger all.

A face-saving device. An expensive shambles. It was the biggest fiasco of the war. "The British were in desperate straits. Russia was demanding that the Dardanelles be forced by the British Navy and Constantinople taken. The Navy could not do it alone and wanted Army support. Kitchener said the British

136

Army had no men available." [*He looks up.*] So what did they do? The Admiralty *insisted* it be done no matter what the risk. Britain's Russian ally was expecting it. There was one solution. Australian and New Zealand troops had just got to Cairo for their initial training. Untrained men, untried. [*He looks quickly back at book.*] "Perhaps they could be used."

[*He snaps the book shut.*] Perhaps. Perhaps they could be pushed in there, into a place everybody knew was impossible to take from the sea, to make the big gesture necessary . . . to save the face of the British. [*He turns on his father.*] . . . the British, Dad, the bloody Poms. THEY pushed those men up those cliffs, that April morning, knowing, KNOWING it was suicide.

You know what it was like. Show them the maps. Show them the photos. A child of six could tell you men with guns on top of those cliffs could wipe out anyone trying to come up from below. And there were guns on top, weren't there, Wacka, weren't there?

Oh yes, great credit to them – if you happen to see any credit in men wasting their lives.

And as long as men like you are fools enough to accept that, to say that, there'll always be wars.

It was doomed from the start, it was a waste! Every year you still march down that street with that stupid proud expression on your face you glorify the – bloody wastefulness of that day.

Believe in the men if you want to, they had guts. But the day . . . it's a mug's day.

The Season at Sarsaparilla

Patrick White

Currency, Sydney 1992

ROY:

They're sleeping now. In the brick boxes. In the brick homes. Their dreams are rubbing on one another. There's nothing like friction, even in a dream. Sometimes they call out . . . and nobody answers. It's terrible then. But is it worse than when a man forgets the language others speak by daylight? It's most terrible of all not to be able to change love into the currency of words.

I've been sitting alone in the kitchen, writing the book I've got to write. Or have I . . . got to? Have I anything to say? Of course I have! Otherwise, *I* would not be *I*. It's only a question of somebody else cracking the code. And somebody must. There's no code that's never been cracked. But till they find the key there are all those torn-up pages . . . so many dead intentions. Life in the brick boxes is never so dead as the ghosts of words littering the kitchen floor.

There are times, and places, when night itself is the ghost of what it's meant to be. Here where the owls no longer float, the air won't let their feathers rest. The great trees continue to spread, never quite exorcized. And soon, we can expect the dawn . . . the least substantial moment of all . . . here where the peewees have died of Thalrat, and teeth grind in the tumblers at thought of another day . . .

The Ham Funeral

Patrick White   Currency, Sydney 1965

Act 1

YOUNG MAN:

[*yawning, addressing the audience*] I have just woken, it seems. It is about . . . well, the time doesn't matter. The same applies to my origins. It could be that I was born in Birmingham . . . or Brooklyn . . . or Murwillumbah. What *is* important is that, thanks to a succession of meat pies (the gristle-and-gravy, cardboard kind) and many cups of pink tea, I am *alive!* Therefore . . . and this is the rather painful point . . . I must go in soon and take part in the play, which, as usual, is a piece about eels. As I am also a poet . . . though, to be perfectly honest, I have not yet found out for sure . . . my dilemma in the play is how to take part in the conflict of eels, and survive at the same time . . . becoming a kind of Roman candle . . . fizzing for ever in the dark. [*Somewhat stern*] Probably quite a number of you are wondering by now whether this is your kind of play. I'm sorry to have to announce the management won't refund any money. You must simply sit it out, and see whether you can't recognize some of the forms that will squirm before you in this mad, muddy mess of eels. As it heaves and shudders, you may even find . . . you have begun to feed . . . on memory . . . [*more relaxed, as if returning to his private world*] Let me remind you of a great, damp, crumbling house in which people are living. Remember? Perhaps you have only dreamt it. Some of the doors of the house have never been seen open. The people whose protection they are intended to ensure can be heard bumping about behind them. Sometimes these characters fry little meals for their temporary comfort. Sometimes it sounds as though they are breaking glass. As far as we know, nobody has ever committed a murder in this house of ours, but it could be . . . [*slowing up, thoughtfully*] Certainly murder has often been contemplated . . . [*looking at his wrist-watch*] . . . towards five

139

o'clock . . . when the fingers have turned to bones . . . and the sky is green. There are the voices, too. Not only the voices of the walls. There are the voices of the gas-fires, full of advice that we haven't the courage to take. And the mirrors in the deal dressing-tables . . . well, you can never believe *them*. They are living lies, down to the last vein in their eyeballs. So, we turn our backs. But look again. The landlady, you're going to see, spends an awful lot of here time looking again. And I . . . but I know already. I know too much. That is the poet's tragedy. To know too much, and never enough. [*Defensive*] You are right in suspecting I can't give you a message. The message always gets torn up. It lies at the bottom of the basket, under the hair, and everything else. Don't suggest we piece it together. I've found the answer is always different. So . . . the most I can do is give you the play, and plays, of course, are only plays. Even the great play of life. Some of you will argue that *that* is real enough . . . [*very quiet and diffident*] . . . but can we be . . . sure? [*Returning to the surface, dry*] Thank you. We'd better begin now.

What if You Died Tomorrow

David Williamson

Currency, Sydney 1991

HARRY:

I'd never take you to court over this. You know that. If O'Hearn advises you to take Chisolms' offer and you take his advice, then that's it as far as I'm concerned. No hard feelings. And I'm sorry about pulling that loyalty bullshit. You don't owe me anything. I took on your work because it was good. No other reason. Because it was good, and if there's one damned thing I can do and do well it's spot quality. I am a talent sniffer. That's it. That's me. Pure and simple. A talent sniffer and I can sniff it out better than anyone else in this country, and consider this, consider this, boy. Talent is a commodity just like anything else, it's a commodity that's got to be found and mined and processed, and I found you and I mined you and I processed you for one reason and for one reason only – because I knew you were good and because I knew that if I treated you fairly and honestly you would make us both a fortune one day. That's the reason I've always been straight with you. Not any phoney honesty or principles or any of that crap. Because you were good, and I knew that if I did anything sharp or shady or tricksy with you, sooner or later you would find out and say, "Up you, Harry," and there would go my golden goose flying right out of the window. Get me? So forgive me for peddling that loyalty bullshit. All I've done for you I've done out of pure self-interest. My Christ. I've been dishonest in my time. I could tell you some things I've done that I'm still ashamed of, but never to you, boy. Never, never to you, and it's not that I'm patting myself on the back, as I've said a few times already, it's out of pure self-interest.

The Club

David Williamson

Currency, Sydney 1978

GEOFF:

Have I ever talked to you about my sister?

I don't speak about her very often. She was in a serious car accident the night before her eighteenth birthday. I was only fourteen.

Both legs were amputated above the knee.

It would've been tragic for anyone – but for someone as young and beautiful as Gabrielle it was shattering. She wasn't just beautiful either, Jock; she was intelligent, warm, cheerful, popular – she had everything going for her. We tried to keep a stiff lip but I was distraught and so were my parents. Every time I looked at her I had to turn my head away so that she wouldn't see me cry, because the last thing she wanted was pity. I just can't tell you how brave she was, Jock. Don't be sad, she'd say. I'm still alive and I've still got my family. I mean Jesus, is that courage, Jock, Is it?

You're looking a bit pale.

So I went and lay beside her and held her in my arms and we cried together. For hours. Every night after that I'd comfort her in the same way and we'd lie together crying in the dark, then one night . . . I'm sorry Jock, I shouldn't inflict this story on anyone. You're looking as white as a sheet.

Are you sure it's not getting too heavy?

Well, without either of us knowing quite how or why, we became lovers.

We knew what we were doing was wrong. The surprising thing was that we didn't care. It all seemed so right. Can you understand that, Jock? It was wrong but it was right. Can you understand that?

It sounds sordid but it wasn't. I loved her, Jock.

One night when Dad was away on one of his many business

trips the light was suddenly switched on and there was my mother.

Can you imagine how we felt? Can you imagine how she felt? I can still see her standing there. Still young, and still beautiful in a flowing silk negligee and with a look of utter shock on her face. There was nothing she could say to us and there was nothing we could say to her. She turned off the light and went back to her room and we clung together listening to her sobbing. Finally I couldn't stand it any longer. I picked up my sister and carried her to Mother's room and we all clung together crying like lost souls in the dark. Gradually as the night wore on . . . this is too much for you, isn't it, Jock?

It gets worse.

Again, I've no idea quite how and why but my mother and I became lovers too.

Three nights later my father arrived home early from a conference.

He looked at the three of us and said just one thing. "You've killed me, son." Three days later he shot himself. I've been impotent ever since.

A Handful of Friends

David Williamson   Currency, Sydney 1976

MARK:

She's got plenty of spirit, hasn't she?

I like a woman who stands up for herself. She's alive, Russell. Really alive. You've no idea what a difference she's made to me. I like a woman who stands up for herself and gives me something to bounce off. Her only problem is that she's ambitious. She wants to be someone. "Why?" I keep asking her. Look at me. I'm someone and look at me. So screwed up it isn't funny. A competitive society has a built-in and fundamental contradiciton. It encourages you to fight your way to prominence and as soon as you succeed it sends out the hatchet men to carve you up again, piece by piece. Jesus, they've crucified me over this latest picture of mine, Russell. I keep a brave face in public, but there's a lot of weeping in private. God, they've made a mess of me. There's no need for me to tell you how glad I am that you're back.

I mean it. You don't exactly make friends hand over fist in my game and it leaves a big hole in your defences when your best friend goes overseas for seven years.

It's a good movie. Utterly competent. God, Russell, they're like wolves. Every time a young director makes a film that isn't literally falling apart at the seams they hail the bastard as my successor. There's a hunger for novelty out there that's absolutely insatiable. God knows how any man can cope with it. I can't. I'm shot through with arthritis, can't sleep at night – all that kind of scene. Creators are the sacrificial objects of a bored society. I'll be dead in five years.

It's true. I'm done for. If I had any sense I'd get out and buy a houses on a cliff overlooking the ocean and watch the waves pounding Christ out of the rocks, but I can't. The adrenalin keeps pounding in my arteries and every time I get kicked in the face I get up for more. I'm going to make one good film before I die. It's the only motive I've got left. One good film before I die and it's going to be so good that none of those bitter little typewriter assassins will dare knock it. It's going to be this one, Russell. I haven't said it to anyone else yet, so mark these words, they're historic, *it's going to be this one!* . . .

It's my film, Russell. It's my destiny and I'm ready for it. I am ready for it.

Emerald City

David Williamson

Currency, Sydney 1987

Act 1

COLIN:

[*suddenly, passionately*] What's happening is that I'm getting older and I'm starting to have the nightmare that every writer gets: ending my life as a deadbeat, flogging scripts to producers who don't want 'em. And it's not paranoia. It happens. Henry Lawson was sent to gaol because he couldn't pay his debts. Ended his life begging in the streets of Sydney and did anyone care? Not one! He'd be really amused today if he could see his head on our ten dollar note. Cultural hero – kids study him in schools – ended his life as a joke and nobody cared! It's not going to happen to me. I'm sick of sending scripts off and waiting patiently for the call that never comes and ringing back and ringing back and finally getting someone on the other end of the phone who says, 'Sorry', they haven't had time to read it yet. Being a writer is one of the most humiliating professions on earth and I'm sick to death of it. I want to be a producer, and I want to have money, and I want to have power. I want to sit in my office with people phoning *me*. I want to sit back and tell my secretary that I'm in conference and can't be disturbed and that I'll ring back, then make sure I never do. I want scripts to come to *me*, and *I'll* make the judgements about whether they're good, bad or indifferent. *I'll* be the one with the blue pencil who rips other people's scripts apart, complains about the banality and predictability, groans at the clichéd dialogue, mutters, 'There must be some good writers *somewhere*'. Why *shouldn't* I have money and power? Why *shouldn't* I have a great big house on the waterfront like all the rest of the coked-out mumblers out there masquerading as producers? I want *you* to stop telling people what *I* want out of *my* life, because you are *wrong*! I don't want to make art films or films with a message, I want to produce a product that entertains and I want it to make me awesomely powerful and fabulously rich!

Act 2

MIKE:

[*into the phone*] Sounds great. Why don't I come around and we'll talk about it?

[*Pause.*]

Yep. That's fine. See you then.

[*He hangs up and notes down the time and place in his diary.*]

[*Exultantly*] Terry Severino wants me to write a movie for him.

When you're hot, you run with it. Next week you might be colder than Melbourne in May.

Honey, it's make or break time. They've thrown me the ball and I've got to run with it.

[*taking tablets*] You want to live in this dump all your life?

Add up the numbers in the contracts I've signed in the last two months and it comes to more than I've earned in the last ten years.

. . .

[*interrupting*] Honey, you are *'un poule superieux'*.

A top chook. You could've had any guy in this city, and don't think I don't know it. I am going to put you in a mansion on the waterfront with a boat moored outside, because anything less is an insult.

. . .

[*interrupting*] Honey, there are women out there with a tenth of what you've got who've treated me like shit. How do you say, 'Thank you' to someone who's given you more than you ever hoped for and much more than you deserve? This is the only way I know how.

Honey, for the first time in my life I've found a game I might win. Suddenly, there's a doorway, and I've got a foot in, and I can see myself through and on the other side and nobody's putting me down any more, and do you know what that's like to me? That's like being in heaven. Bliss.

[HELEN *exits.*]

[*To the audience*] Problem is, when you take on half a dozen big jobs at once, you do eventually have to deliver. I started living on a diet of milk and indigestion tablets and as the

146

telephone calls started coming in my brain log-jammed with fear and dread. No shortage of ideas. Brilliant ideas. But between the idea and the typewriter something happened. There was some freak circuit in my brain that, right at the last moment, in the instant before the idea hit the paper, turned gold into shit. I was in a waking nightmare. I was a grand opera singer who hears the nightingale inside her head, opens her mouth, and out comes the croak of a frog. The phone kept ringing and I extended the dates again, and again. My brain was on the point of exploding. My stomach already had. I looked down, teetering on the brink of the success I'd always dreamed of and saw the crocodiles below. There *had* to be a way out. *Had* to.

Act 2

MIKE:

Malcolm, listen. Let's have a long hard look at this industry of ours. Over four hundred films in the last ten years and only *one* has done big business where it counts: in the U.S.

. . . We've been failing because we've been going about it in a half-arsed way. We bring over a few faded American stars and plonk them in a cliché-ridden Australian wank, and think we've made something international. We'll *never* make true international product that way. We have to go the whole hog. A big production house with ten or twelve projects going at once and *everything* international. International scripts, international stars, international directors. Malcolm, there's no reason why Australia couldn't become one of the world's great production houses. Climates better than California, technicians are much cheaper. Got good local actors for the supporting roles . . .

Malcolm. I swear to you, it can be done. The Canadians make better American movies than the Americans, and the reason they succeed is that they don't feel they have to maker pissant little movies about the Canadian way of life. We'll have all the Advance Aussie patriots having hernia's because we put American numberplates on Aussie cars, but stuff'em, Malcolm.

Stuff'em. If we'd just be honest with ourselves for a change, we'd admit that our accent *is* bloody awful for the simple reason that we never open our bloody mouths. It was good enough in the old days when Grandad was out in the bush and had to keep the flies out, but it's *death* to the international saleability of our product.

You pay expenses to get me to L.A. so I can line up the talent and do the deals. Every project I get up we split the profits fifty-fifty. If I don't get anything up, all you've lost is a few plane fares.

The world's a global village, Malcolm. A merchant banker in New York has got far more in common with you than a sheep farmer from Walgett, right?

Let's start making hard-headed, rational business decisions for a change. The North American market is three hundred million, ours is fifteen. Where does the future lie?

The Revengers' Comedies

Alan Ayckbourn

Faber & Faber, London 1991

ANTHONY:

I could be a lot more unpleasant than this if I tried, I warn you. I can be deeply, deeply unpleasant, chummy, if I choose to be – believe me, so far as you're concerned, at this moment in time, I'm being as charming as you're ever likely to know me, so I should make the best of it. Because I'm not going to be made a public laughing stock by some poncified townie with a hideous taste in suits coming down here and bonking my wife in my own chicken sheds, all right? . . . And what the hell's Karen Knightly been telling you?

　　She and I had – well, you could hardly term it an affair – had a bit of sex together, let's say – for all of a month. Well, quite a lot of sex, really. We tried out all twenty-five of the bedrooms in that house of hers over the course of about a fortnight, starting in the attic and finishing up in the master suite. She insisted we dressed in suitable clothes to suit different locations. I remember our night in the nursery as particularly bizarre. When we'd completed the course, she declared that according to ancient law we were now legally engaged. And that at the next full moon I had to sacrifice my existing wife Imogen and change my name to Alric the Awesome. At which point, I realized she was stark staring mad and I broke off the relationship. She then plagued us both for months. Writing anonymous letters, drawing strange runes on our front door, phoning up claiming to be a midwife delivering my illegitimate child. You name it, she did it. Culminating, finally, in a phone call demanding that I be on Chelsea Bridge at eight thirty sharp or she would throw herself in the Thames.

I stood on that bloody bridge for an hour and a half hoping to see her jump. No such luck. Not so much as a ripple. So I went home again.

Karen Knightly is totally immaterial. I've forgotten her. We're talking about Imogen. And that one you can forget. You keep out of my chickens. Away from my cows. Off my pigs. And well clear of my wife, all right?

Fair Slaughter
Howard Barker

John Calder, London 1978

Scene 14

YOUNG GOCHER:

[*Spotlight on* YOUNG GOCHER, *in overalls, standing on a wooden crate. Pause. He mentally prepares.*]

Comrades . . . Comrades . . . [*Pause.*] The class war is suspended. The patriotic war has begun. [*Pause.*] Yesterday I urged you – break the machines. Yesterday I said – cut through the driving belts, neglect the oilcan, loosen bolts. Yesterday I said – produce only when every obstacle to production is exhausted. Today I say to you – step up the power, sacrifice your teabreak, take time off only when your bladder or your bowels compel you to. Today I say – break records. [*Pause.*] Now why, comrades? Why this apparent about-face? Because you see, I hear you murmuring, I hear your rumbling doubts and queries. Is the boss the enemy, or is he not? [*Pause.*] To which I say, if only life were that simple! Because if life were that simple, we would have been the masters long ago. [*Pause.*] We are inspired by an ideal, an ideal which became reality, an ideal which has shifted the dead weight of history. The ideal of the Soviet Union. But while we are inspired by an ideal, our business is with facts. And today, with one fact in particular. Comrade Stalin, far away in his Kremlin, has especially asked me to acquaint you with this fact. And the fact is, that the Soviet Union has been attacked. [*Pause.*] Now, you do not need me to underline the meaning of that fact. Russia is attacked, the international working class movement is attacked, we are all attacked. [*Pause.*] So we suspend our conflict, our national conflict, in the wider interests of the world socialist movement. We close ranks with the capitalists not out of treason, but from loyalty - loyalty to the International working class. We work our fingers to the bone to defend the citadel of socialism and we discover a new slogan - NO SLACKING IN THE SOCIALIST STRUGGLE! Comrades, to your benches, to your lathes! [*Pause.*] Address to the Extraordinary General Meeting of the Shop Stewards' Committee of the Engineering Union, the Borough, July, 1941.

Red Noses

Peter Barnes   Faber & Faber, London 1985

FIRST ATTENDANT:

Hoo-hooo-ooooh. I've got the boils, the black buboes! I'm stricken. [*The others shrink back.*] Mother of God, I'm not ready. I've only just been born and now I have to die. All the fault of writers - cock-pimping scribblers. They've prepared the way. Always writing stories where some characters are important and others just disposable stock - First Attendant, Second Peasant, Third Guard. Stories're easier when 'tisn't possible to care for everyone equal. That's how itty-bitty-bit people like me come to be butchered on battlefields, die in droves on a *hoo-hoooooooh.* But we First Attendants are important too. We've lives. I've lodged in the chaffinch, lived in the flower, seen the sun coming up. I've discovered unbelievable things. I'm an extraordinary person. I'll tell you a secret . . .

[*He dies.*]

A Chip in the Sugar

Alan Bennett

From *Talking Heads,*
BBC Books, London 1990

GRAHAM:

There must be a famine on somewhere because we were just
letting our midday meal go down when the vicar calls with some
envelopes. Breezes in, anorak and running shoes, and he says, 'I
always look forward to coming to this house, Mrs Whittaker.'
(He's got the idea she's deaf, which she's not; it's one of the few
things she isn't.) He says, 'Do you know why? It's because you
two remind me of Jesus and his mother.' Well, I've always
thought Jesus was a bit off-hand with his mother, and on one
occasion I remember he was quite snotty with her, but I didn't
say anything. And of course Madam is over the moon. In her
book if you can't get compared with the Queen Mother the
Virgin Mary's the next best thing. She says, 'Are you married?'
(She asks him every time, never remembers.) He said, 'No, Mrs
Whittaker. I am married to God.' She says, 'Where does that
leave you with the housework?' He said, 'Well, I don't do as well
as your Graham. He's got this place like a palace.' She says,
'Well, I do my whack. I washed four pairs of stockings this
morning.' She hadn't. She put them in the bowl then they
slipped her mind, so the rest of the operation devolved on me.

He said, 'How are you today, Mrs Whittaker?' She says, 'Stiff
down one side.' I said. 'She had a fall yesterday.' She says, 'I
never did.' I said, 'You did, Mother. You had a fall, then you ran
into Mr Turnbull.'

[*Pause.*]

She says, 'That's right. I did.' And she starts rooting in her bag
for her lipstick. She says, 'That's one of them anoraky things,
isn't it? They've gone out now, those. If you want to look like a
man about town you want to get one of those continental quilts.'
He said, 'Oh?' I said, 'She means those quilted jackets.' She said,

152

'He knows what I mean. Where did you get those shoes?' He said, 'They're training shoes.' She said, 'Training for what? Are you not fully qualified?' He said, 'If Jesus were alive today, Mrs Whittaker, I think you'd find these were the type of shoes he would be wearing.' 'Not if his mother had anything to do with it,' she said. 'She'd have him down Stead and Simpson's and get him into some good brogues. Somebody was telling me the Italians make good shoes.'

The vicar takes this as his cue to start on about people who have no shoes at all and via this to the famine in Ethiopia. I fork out 50p which he says will feed six families for a week and she says, 'Well, it would have bought me some Quality Street.' When he's at the door he says, 'I take my hat off to you, Graham, I've got a mother myself.' When I get back in she said, 'Vicar! He looked more like the paper boy. How can you look up to somebody in pumps?'

Decadence

Steven Berkoff
John Calder, London 1981

Scene 6

LES:

Cor blimey, shush / you're putting me off / my mind's ablaze with violent acts inspired by your need for facts / I'll prove I love you / I'll make you see just how wondrous thou art to me / I'll measure my love in deeds so cute / I'll make de Sade go back to school / first of all one night / he comes home / stops the car, alights / my car's just behind and rams him down and pastes him to the side / he needs unpeeling so intense will be my hard caress / in bed one night / he's with his whore / there'll be a little tapping on the door / he, careful as a skunk thinking his trail has left no trace of stink / peeps through the spyhole / and sees me /

153

costumed as a telegram boy / all safe he thinks and opens up / a ten inch blade dives in his gut / at his squash club / he's had his game / all sweaty in his shower / innocent and tame / in the stream no one sees a furtive me drop a tarantula in his pants / he dries off / dresses and suddenly shrieks / there's something up his kyber pass and it feels to me like broken glass / 'cause tarantula bite is a vicious sight / or a bomb under the lovers' bed / ready to go off as she or he comes / a neat device so sensitive / that extra pressure will blow them to shreds / they'll fly / that's an orgasm that will send them to paradise / gun's too messy and far too noisy / let's leave that out and choose a poison / we'll send him a Christmas cake juiced up with cyanide / lots of sherry to help disguise the bitter acrid taste that burns his guts / she'll scream in pain / they'll wait as death starts digging inside their brain / or, excuse me, what's the time? hydrochloric acid in his eyes / he screams / then in the dark / a fine needle penetrates his heart / he didn't see it / so in his dying breath he cannot identify Mr. Death / a minute atomic bomb the size of a pearl / a present in a ring from his golden girl timed to go off whenever you will / as the mood takes you ka boom ka blast ke pling! In Africa from leper colony I extract from a native a deadly smear / then lace his shaver / one morning you'll hear / Oh I've scratched myself darling / smile and count down the minutes my dear / best of all I'll loose some rats whose fangs have been dipped in a deadly unction / one small bite and the cunt won't function / longer than it takes to drop down dead / it also saves disposing of the corpse since the rats will eat the lot of course / so whatyathink – you make your choice dove / it's just to show you what I feel is love! . . .

Pull off your drawers

Greek

Steven Berkoff

John Calder, London 1983

Scene 3

EDDY:

She would put you off women for life / but not me / I love a woman / I love her / I just love and love and love her / and even that one / I could have loved her / I love everything that they possess / I love all their parts / I love every part that moves / I love their hair and their neck / I love the way they walk across the kitchen to put the kettle on / in that lazy familiar way / I love them when they open their eyes in the morning / I love their baby soft skin / I love their voices / I love their smaller hands than mine / I love lying on them and them on me / I love their soft breasts / I love their eyelashes and their noses / their teeth and their shoulders / and their giggles / and their desperate passions and their liquids and their breath against yours in the night / and their snores / and their leg across yours and their feet in the morning and I love their bellies and thighs and the way each part fits into mine / and love the way my part fits into them / and love her sockets and joints and ball bearings / and love her hip bone and her love soaked parts that want me / I love her seasons and her sleeping and love her walking and speaking and whispering and loving and singing and love her back and her bum nestled into you and you become an armchair / and love her for taking me in / and giving me a home for my searing agonies / my lusts / my love / my dreams / my sweetness / my honey / my peace of mind / and love pouring all my love into her with open eyes and love our fatigue and love her knees and shoulder blades and pimples and love her waiting for me / and love her soothing me as I tell her about my day's battles in the world / and love and love and love her and her and!

155

The Cagebirds

David Campton
Samuel French, London 1976

Scene 1

WILD ONE:

All right. Let me try to put myself in your place. How long have you been here? Days? Weeks? Months? Years? Have you always been here? Are you content to sit as time slips by – all the days, weeks, months, years to come? She said you're content. Perhaps you are. But if you are it's because you never . . . Doesn't anything matter to you beyond aches and food, scandal and the reflection in your mirror? Isn't there room for anything in your mind but prejudice and fear? You're oppressed and you don't even notice the fact. You are denied your basic human rights, and you don't even care. You are prisoners. Are you content with that? I'm just trying to understand you, that's all. Just trying. Did you ever behave like me? Did you ever beat at the door, shout protest slogans? Complain about the injustice of it all? Or shall I, given time, become like you – secure in my own little space, perhaps working out endless, beautiful, complicated, useless plans for escape? Never! Listen to me. You are going to listen to me.

Listen. The world stretches farther than the few inches between your ears. Out there where the wind blows and the sun shines. Where heat and light and air have nothing to do with central heating or electric lamps or air conditioning. Do you remember the wind? It tickles and it buffets; it sighs and it roars; it swoops suddenly from the north tearing trees in its path; then, just as suddenly, it changes into a whisper from the south, rustling in the grass. That's the wind. Can you live without it? Of course you can – as long as you can forget about it.

I'm reminding you again. I don't want to hurt you. But does it hurt so much to remember? Do you remember the clouds? Little white puffs against a wash of blue; great, grey mountains piling up until they crash in thunder; fiery streamers of flame

156

and gold blazing across the sky in the hallelujah of a sunset. The clouds. Remember them? Those high-bourne miracles. Remember?

You must remember. Remember the winter. Yes, even the frost. When every pool became a mirror and every spray a crystal cluster. When the earth set rock hard, and each day was a test with bare life the prize at the end. When owls hooted at the frozen moon, and hawks plummeted down the thin air. Yes, remember even hunger and death. But can you remember that and be content with this?

Don't you want to escape – even into memories? Please. Unwind. I'm trying to help. I want to set you free. [*Pause*] That wasn't the way either.

Where did I fail? Am I too articulate? Should I have limited my words, scaled down my imagination to your mind. I can't. I would if I could because I want to reach you. But I can't. You're all out of reach.

Ivanov

Anton Chekhov Penguin, London 1973

Act 4

IVANOV:

If I could sneer at myself a thousand times harder and set the whole world laughing, then sneer I would. I looked at myself in the glass and something seemed to snap inside me. I laughed at myself and nearly went out of my mind with shame. [*Laughs.*] ... To see that some people think you're a fraud, others feel sorry for you, yet others hold out a helping hand, while a fourth lot – worst of all – listen to your sighs with reverence, looking on you as a great prophet and expecting you to preach a new religion! No, I still have some pride and conscience, thank God. I laughed

157

at myself on my way here, and I felt as though the very birds were laughing at me, and the trees.

No, I'm not mad. I see things in their true light now, and my thoughts are as innocent as your own. We love each other, but our marriage is not to be. I can rant and fret to my heart's content, but I've no right to destroy anyone else. I poisoned the last year of my wife's life with my snivelling. Since we've been engaged you've forgotten how to laugh, and you look five years older. And your father, who once had a pretty sane outlook, can't make sense of people any more, thanks to me. When I attend meetings, go visiting or shooting – I carry boredom, gloom and despondency everywhere. No, don't interrupt. I'm being brutally frank, but I'm in a rotten temper, sorry, and this is the only way I can speak . . .

Once an intelligent, educated, healthy man begins feeling sorry for himself for no obvious reason and starts rolling down the slippery slope, he rolls on and on without stopping and nothing can save him. Well, where is there hope for me? What could it be? I can't drink, spirits make my head ache. I can't write bad verse, nor can I worship my own mental laziness and put it on a pedestal. Laziness is laziness, weakness is weakness – I can't find other names for them. I'm done for, I tell you, there's no more to be said. [*Looks round.*] We might be interrupted. Listen. If you love me, help me. You must break off the marriage without delay – this very instant. Hurry up . . .

. . . You set yourself to rescue me at all costs and make a new man of me, and you liked to think you were being heroic. Now you're ready to back out, but sentimentality stands in your way, don't you see? . . .

I was a fool to come here, I should have done as I intended.

Act 4 Scene 10

IVANOV:

Listen, my poor man. I won't try and explain myself – whether I'm decent or rotten, sane or mad. You wouldn't understand. I used to be young, eager, sincere, intelligent. I loved, hated and believed differently from other people, I worked hard enough – I had hope enough – for ten men. I tilted at windmills and banged my head against brick walls. Without measuring my own strength, taking thought or knowing anything about life, I heaved a load on my back which promptly tore the muscles and cracked my spine. I was in a hurry to expend all my youthful energy, drank too much, got over-excited, worked, never did things by halves. But tell me, what else could you expect? We're so few, after all, and there's such a lot to be done, God knows. And now look how cruelly life, the life I challenged, is taking its revenge. I broke under the strain. I woke up to myself at the age of thirty, I'm like an old man in his dressing-gown and slippers. Heavy-headed, dull-witted, worn out, broken, shattered, without faith or love, with no aim in life, I moon around, more dead than alive, and don't know who I am, what I'm living for or what I want. Love's a fraud, or so I think, and any show of affection's just sloppy sentimentality, there's no point in working, songs and fiery speeches are cheap and stale. Wherever I go I carry misery, indifference, boredom, discontent and disgust with life. I'm absolutely done for. You see a man exhausted at the age of thirty-five, disillusioned, crushed by his own pathetic efforts, bitterly ashamed of himself, sneering at his own feebleness. How my pride rebels, I'm choking with fury. [*Staggering.*] God, I'm on my last legs – I'm so weak I can hardly stand. Where's Matthew? I want him to take me home.

The Three Sisters

Anton Chekhov

Act 3

ANDREY:

You're the person I'm looking for. Give me the key to the cupboard, will you – I've lost mine. You know that little key you've got.

[OLGA *silently gives him the key.* IRINA *goes to her own corner behind the screen.*]

[*Pause.*]

What an enormous fire, though! It's begun to die down now. Damn it, he made me so cross, that man Ferapont. That was a stupid thing I said to him . . . Making him call me sir.

[*Pause.*]

Why don't you say something, then, Olya?

[*Pause.*]

It's time you stopped all this nonsense. It's time you stopped pouting about like that for no earthly reason. You're here, Masha. Irina's here. All right, then, let's have it out in the open, once and for all. What have you three got against me? What is it? . . .

You've got something against Natasha, my wife too, and this I've been aware of from the very day we got married. Natasha is a fine person – honest, straightforward, and upright – that's my opinion. I love and respect my wife – I respect her, you understand? – and I insist that others respect her, too. I say it again – she is an honest and upright person, and all your little marks of displeasure – forgive me, but you're simply behaving like spoilt children.

[*Pause.*]

Secondly, you seem to be angry that I'm not a professor, that I'm not a scientist. But I serve in local government, I am a member of the local Council, and this service I consider just as sacred, just as elevated, as any service I could render to science.

I am a member of the local Council and proud of it, if you wish to know . . .

[*Pause.*]

Thirdly . . . I have something else to say . . . I mortgaged the house without asking your permission . . . To this I plead guilty, and indeed I ask you to forgive me . . . I was driven to it by my debts . . . thirty-five thousand . . . I don't play cards now – I gave it up long since – but the main thing I can say in my own justification is that you're girls, and you get an annuity, whereas I had no . . . well, no income . . .

[*Pause*]

They're not listening. Natasha is an outstanding woman, someone of great integrity.

[*Walks about in silence, then stops.*]

When I got married I thought we were going to be happy . . . all going to be happy . . . But my God . . . [*Weeps.*] My dear sisters, my own dear sisters, don't believe me, don't trust me . . . [*He goes.*]

Strife

John Galsworthy Gerald Duckworth, London 1958

Act 2 Scene 2

ROBERTS:

We have not much to thank Mr. Harness and the Union for.
They said to us "Desert your mates, or we'll desert you." An'
they did desert us.

Mr. Simon Harness is a clever man, but he has come too late.
[*With intense conviction.*] For all that Mr. Simon Harness says,
for all that Thomas, Rous, for all that any man present here can
say – *We've won the fight!*

[*The crowd sags nearer, looking eagerly up. With withering
scorn.*]

You've felt the pinch o't in your bellies. You've forgotten what
that fight 'as been; many times I have told you; I will tell you
now this once again. The fight o' the country's body and blood
against a blood-sucker. The fight of those that spend themselves
with every blow they strike and every breath they draw, against a
thing that fattens on them, and grows and grows by the law of
merciful Nature. That thing is Capital! A thing that buys the
sweat o' men's brows, and the tortures o' their brains, at its own
price. *Don't I* know that? Wasn't the work o' *my* brains bought for
seven hundred pounds, and hasn't one hundred thousand
pounds been gained them by that seven hundred without the
stirring of a finger? It is a thing that will take as much and give
you as little as it can. That's *Capital!* A thing that will say – "I'm
very sorry for you, poor fellows – you have a cruel time of it, I
know," but will not give one sixpence of its dividends to help you
have a better time. That's Capital! Tell me, for all their talk is
there one of them that will consent to another penny on the
Income Tax to help the poor? That's Capital! A white-faced,
stony-hearted monster! Ye have got it on its knees; are ye to give
up at the last minute to save your miserable bodies pain? When I
went this morning to those old men from London, I looked into

162

their very 'earts. One of them was sitting there – Mr. Scantle-bury, a mass of flesh nourished on us: sittin' there for all the world like the shareholders in this Company, that sit not moving tongue nor finger, takin' dividends – a great dumb ox that can only be roused when its food is threatened. I looked into his eyes and I saw *he was afraid* – afraid for himself and his dividends, afraid for his fees, afraid of the very shareholders he stands for; and all but one of them's afraid – like children that get into a wood at night, and start at every rustle of the leaves. I ask you, men –

[*he pauses, holding out his hand till there is utter silence*]

Give me a free hand to tell them: "Go you back to London. The men have nothing for you!"

[*A murmuring.*]

Give me that, an' I swear to you, within a week you shall have from London all you want.

'Tis not for this little moment of time we're fighting [*the murmuring dies*], not for ourselves, our own little bodies, and their wants, 'tis for all those that come after throughout all time. [*With intense sadness.*] Oh! men – for the love o' them, don't roll up another stone upon their heads, don't help to blacken the sky, an' let the bitter sea in over them. They're welcome to the worst that can happen to me, to the worst that can happen to us all, aren't they – aren't they? If we can shake [*passionately*] that white-faced monster with the bloody lips, that has sucked the life out of ourselves, our wives and children, since the world began. [*Dropping the note of passion, but with the utmost weight and intensity.*] If we have not the hearts of men to stand against it breast to breast, and eye to eye, and force it backward till it cry for mercy, it will go on sucking life; and we shall stay for ever what we are, [*in almost a whisper*] less than the very dogs.

[*An utter stillness, and* ROBERTS *stands rocking his body slightly, with his eyes burning the faces of the crowd.*]

"Nature," says that old man, "give in to Nature." *I* can tell you, strike your blow in Nature's face – an' let it do its worst!

Act 2, Scene 2

HARNESS:

Now, men, be reasonable. Your demands would have brought on us the burden of a dozen strikes at a time when we were not prepared for them. The Unions live by Justice, not to one, but all. Any fair man will tell you – you were ill-advised! I don't say you go too far for that which you're entitled to, but you're going too far for the moment; you've dug a pit for yourselves. Are you to stay there, or are you to climb out? Come!

[*Another movement in the crowd, and* ROUS, *coming quickly, takes his stand next to* THOMAS.]

Cut your demands to the right pattern, and we'll see you through; refuse, and don't expect me to waste my time coming down here again. I'm not the sort that speaks at random, as you ought to know by this time. If you're the sound men I take you for – no matter who advises you against it – [*he fixes his eyes on* ROBERTS] you'll make up your minds to come in, and trust to us to get your terms. Which is it to be? Hands together, and victory – or – the starvation you've got now?

[*A prolonged murmur from the crowd.*]

[*With cold passion*] All that you've been through, my friend, I've been through – I was through it when I was no bigger than [*pointing to a youth*] that shaver there; the Unions then weren't what they are now. What's made them strong? It's hands to-gether that's made them strong. I've been through it all, I tell you, the brand's on my soul yet. I know what you've suffered – there's nothing you can tell me that I don't know; but the whole is greater than the part, and you are only the part. Stand by us, and we will stand by you.

[*Quartering them with his eyes, he waits.*]

164

A Month in the Country

Simon Gray

Faber & Faber, London 1990

MOON:

I half wanted it to happen. There were times when I'd had enough. Well, you know that. I mean – when I was sure my nerve would give way and I'd lie down before I was hit. Or worse. Wouldn't be able to drive myself over the top, ever again. So many had gone. Chaps I cared for. Sometimes it seemed they were the lucky ones. [*Pause.*] The night's the bad time. Well, I expect you've heard me. I still wake up screaming. I can still see . . . still see . . . [*pause*] but I tell myself it'll be better as time passes and it sinks further back. But it's got nowhere to sink to, has it? We'll always be different, won't we, the whole lot of us? [*Little pause.*] All the millions of us that survived. If millions did. Different, I mean, from the generations before us who had no idea that anything like that could ever happen. I don't know if it's worse not having something to show for it. Like a lost limb or two or blindness. I mean, people like you and me, the intact ones. The worse part for me was the last part when I was kept away from the fighting. Went for months without seeing a single corpse. The faces I did see – [*stops*] – but I'm a little round the bend, you know. Always will be, I expect. [*Suddenly cheerful*] Still, there's no point in letting it get one down. One's got a life to lead anyway. [*Grins.*] 'And then he shal come with wondes rede to deme the quikke and the dede.'

165

Piano

Trevor Griffiths   Faber & Faber, London 1990

PLATONOV:

I came across a story recently, I don't remember where. Quite a short one, but rather good. About a girl who fell in love with a student, he with her. He'd read books to her, she loved to listen. Sometimes, at dusk, they'd go down to the river and watch the lights of the boats pass by. They sang together, dreamed, kissed swore their love . . .

[*The table listens in silence.* SOPHIA *takes more wine,* SASHENKA *scans faces, uneasy again.*]

The girl wore her hair long then, below her ears, and always on her skin the smell of spring water, and life for them both seemed to unfold like some unending festival . . . dedicated by a kind world to honour their love. And they were happy. One day, she told him she had to go to St Petersburg for a couple of days. 'Do I have your leave!' she asked him. 'Of course,' he answered, 'but you will be missed . . .'

[SOPHIA *stands carefully, glass in hand, stares into the darkness at the storyteller.*]

She took the midnight train, he saw her off at the station, she hugged him tenderly, he squeezed her hands and spoke not a word, scared he would weep. He watched the tail-lights dwindling, mile after mile, and whispered, 'My dear good girl. My wondrous woman.'

[*Pause.*]

A day passed. Two. Five. A month. She didn't come back. The student kept watch at the station, met trains, drank vodka in the station bar. Finally he stopped going. Came to his senses. Grew up. Became an ordinary person.

[PLATONOV *sits, his face averted. Long silence.* SOPHIA *drains her wine, gazes around her, as if trapped.*]

166

PLATONOV:

Wait. Listen. For Christ's sake, woman, hear me out. Please . . .

[*She stops, half turns. He gulps for air. They stare at each other across the ghostly space.*]

Dear wonderful woman . . . My life's gone, I know it, but yours? What's become of *you*? Mm? Where's that . . . simplicity and . . . spirit, unh? Where has all that gone to . . . ?

All right, I'm out of control . . . but be honest with me, in the name of what we once had, why did you marry this man?

He's a *nothing*, and you know it . . .

You could have married *anyone*. You could have married someone with drive and courage and imagination, instead you choose a pygmy, soused in debt and paralytically idle. Why, my love? Why?

How I loved you. My God, how I loved you . . .

[*Another great explosion, another great flare of spectral light washing the space. She turns, moves towards him; he wraps her tight in his arms.*]

[*Low, tiny voice*] Dear good girl. Wondrous woman. You know my problem? I believed in an afterwards. And life doesn't deal in such things. We kid ourselves that everything's still up ahead, waiting to be discovered, waiting to be lived, never mind what we do *now*, there's always 'later', there's always an 'afterwards' to put it right . . . And there isn't. There isn't. Back then . . . I didn't know that. I watched your train disappear . . . I *let* your train disapapear. And . . .

[*They move slowly into a kiss. At the point of closure, she pulls back with a tiny yelp. PLATONOV follows her gaze: sees SERGEI, cloak over arm, watching from a distance. Silence.*]

167

Little Malcolm and His Struggle Against the Eunuchs

David Halliwell   Faber & Faber, London 1967

Scene 6

SCRAWDYKE:

[*Lights up. Dark outside.* SCRAWDYKE *is pacing about.*]
Monday morning. Monday morning already. I've got to have another go at Ann tonight. Oh it's got t' be better than last Friday's 'eroic performance. Got down to 'er place, didn't even manage t' get through t' garden gate. If I 'adn't bumped into 'er as I scuttled away I wouldn't 'ave even seen 'er. Told 'er all about the Party, worked meself into a frenzy. And what did she say? "Sounds difficult." That was it. That was 'er reaction. That's the tremendous impact I made! Now come on. It's no use cryin' over spilled – Scrawdyke. I've got to work this out. Now – well she 'as t' walk up Princess Street. That's 'er quickest way t' trolley stop in front o' t' Co-op. Suppose she comes – There's only one other way she can get there, on Buxton Road. Yes, I know, I can 'ide in that tunnel by Whitfield's shop. One end looks down on Princess Street t' other end comes out on Buxton Road. So I'm in the tunnel. [*He acts this out.*]
   So I watch down – Then I run up t' t' other end. I keep a constant watch. One way – then t' other. I see 'er comin' – say up Princess Street, that's most likely. I watch 'er walk up. She might see me! No, no, it's dark. Lurk man lurk. Right I watch 'er. She comes up past. Suppose she's got somebody wi' 'er. Oh they'll leave 'er go t' t' stop. What if a trolley comes and picks 'er up before I can get there? Oh well, that can't be 'elped. It's unlikely, unlikely, unlikely. So I see 'er – then I come out. Walk on towards 'er casual, just walkin', upright, dignified. An' when I get by 'er, I just see 'er, by accident. What if I falter? I won't. I see

168

'er – "Ah, hullo. Just come up from Tech? I'm just on me way back to the Studio. Been out for a bit of a stroll y' know. Look why don't y' pop in for a cup o' tea if y're not doin' anything. You invited me down t' your place an' I'd like t' return the compliment. It's not exactly a pent'ouse but it 'as one or two amusin' features."

Get 'er in 'ere. Sit 'er down. Fire. Tea. Record. Then – Tell 'er. Yes. Explain. I need 'er. I want 'er. I'm shy – Oh I c'n do it. The right atmosphere. I'm a remarkable man. She'll soon see that. Once she understands, I'm away. The's not really anything t' stop me. The 'ole thing's organic. I shall triumph.

Total Eclipse

Christopher Hampton   Faber & Faber, London 1969

RIMBAUD:

When I was in Paris in February this year, when everything was in a state of chaos, I was staying the night in a barracks and I was sexually assaulted by four drunken soldiers. It wasn't a particularly agreeable experience, but when I got back to Charleville, thinking about it, I began to realize how valuable it had been to me. It clarified things in my mind which had been vague. It gave my imagination textures. And I understood that what I needed, to be the first poet of this century, the first poet since Racine or since the Greeks, was to experience everything in my body. I knew what it was like to be a model pupil, top of the class, now I wanted to disgust them instead of pleasing them. I knew what it was like to take communion, I wanted to take drugs. I knew what it was like to be chaste, I wanted perversions. It was no longer enough for me to be one person, I decided to be everyone. I decided to be a genius. I decided to be Christ. I decided to originate the future.

The fact that I often regarded my ambition as ludicrous and pathetic pleased me, it was what I wanted, contrast, conflict inside my head, that was good. While other writers looked at themselves in the mirror, accepted what they saw, and jotted it down, I liked to see a mirror in the mirror, so that I could turn round whenever I felt like it and always find endless vistas of myself.

However, what I say is immaterial, it's what I write that counts.

RIMBAUD:

When I was young and golden and infallible, I saw the future with some clarity. I saw the failings of my predecessors and saw, I

170

thought, how they could be avoided. I knew it would be difficult, but I thought that all I needed was experience, and I could turn myself into the philosopher's stone, and create new colours and new flowers, new languages and a new God, and everything to gold. Thou shalt, I said to myself, adopting the appropriate apocalyptic style, be reviled and persecuted as any prophet, but at the last thou shalt prevail.

But before long I realized it was impossible to be a doubting prophet. If you are a prophet you may be optimistic or pessimistic as the fancy takes you, but you may never be anything less than certain. And I found I had tortured myself and punished my brain and poked among my entrails to discover something that people do not believe, or do not wish to believe, or would be foolish to believe. And with the lyricism of self-pity, I turned to the mirror and said Lord, what shall I do, for there is no love in the world and no hope, and I can do nothing about it, God, I can do no more than you have done, and I am in Hell, tormented by laughter and locked in the sterility of paradox.

Not that I haven't said all this before.

I have, and clearly a new code is called for. And in these last few weeks when you may have been thinking, I've just been lying here in a state of paralysed sloth, you've actually been quite right. But bubbling beneath the surface and rising slowly through the layers of indifference has been a new system. Harden up. Reject romanticism. Abandon rhetoric. Get it right.

And now I've got it right and seen where my attempt to conquer the world has led me.

Here. My search for universal experience has led me here. To lead an idle, pointless life of poverty, as the minion of a bald, ugly, ageing, drunken lyric poet, who clings on to me because his wife won't take him back.

It's the truth. You're here, living like this, because you have to be. It's your life. Drink and sex and a kind of complacent melancholy and enough money to soak yourself oblivious every night. That's your limit. But I'm here because I choose to be.

The Great Exhibition

David Hare Faber & Faber, London 1972

HAMMETT:

Maud was an actress, will you believe it, the first professional I'd met. She'd been to a school where some plastered dike had taught her the golden rule of the theatre, which was – get out there and glitter. Good advice. Maud would run on the first six steps, come to a dead halt, wobble, flutter her eyelashes, hit an unnaturally high note as if calling a dog at eighty paces, lend a perfectly equal emphasis to every tortured syllable, and then smile at the end of each sentence. Smile and wobble. She was lovely. Best of all as Cordelia. The only smiling and wobbling Cordelia. I loved particularly the glazed expression the whole company had. Witch hazel painted on their eyeballs or something. But not just that. It was that they looked all the time into the distance, desperately avoiding each other's eyes, as if there was some danger that if two of them actually acknowledged each other some terrible kind of contact might happen and the whole performance be ruined. If an actor had the line, "Look into my eyes", you could actually see the shutters come down behind his eyeballs. The man who was playing Lear opposite Maud, and I mean dead opposite Maud, arrived at rehearsals with some charts under his arm. He then laid them out on the stage and retraced the very moves Sir Barry Jackson had used with the Birmingham Repertory Company in 1924. The moves turned out to have a kind of triangular zest. I loved it. It seemed to me at the time that the theatre put to good use could be the most sophisticated possible means of ignoring what people were actually like.

HAMMETT:

It's not just that I'm boring, though I am, very boring, but that I'm a carrier as well. Boredom spreads round me like contagion.

In perfectly cheerful rooms people begin to fidget and to fart. So not only am I not entertaining, also I am rarely entertained. I have to keep trying to catch groups of people off guard, slip in when they're not looking in the hope they haven't noticed I've arrived, so that for a few moments I can watch normal people smiling and amusing each other, before some scrupulous lout starts to sniff and turns to the door and notices me, and then – well – even if it were Oscar Wilde he'd say, sorry I can't actually remember the end of my story, I've got a terrible headache, and the epigram would just be left there hanging, like some blunted icicle. That's the effect I have. Have you noticed?

I'm spectacularly boring. I know something about it. It's not a matter of being funny – I can get my tongue round some pretty acute phrases, you know, jokes. It's just I make everyone uneasy. They can't relax. Parliament's the only place I've ever felt at home.

They're all shell-shock victims, all life's walking wounded, putting a reasonable front on things. I go and gossip and feel at ease, and excuse myself by being rude about the place. . . .

I fear these events – this evening – what I fear –

I fear tonight's the real beginning of my parliamentary career, not the end. The idea was – back there – if I can do this I can do anything.

[*Pause*]

Smell the air.

. . .

The ground I've trodden on for ten years has shifted away and I'm conscious of talking in the air. I can't even mouth the word "revolution" any longer. It sounds so limp and second-hand. Those of us who believed that the world would get better have been brought up short. The thing gets worse not just because of what happens, but because the weight of knowledge of what *ought* to happen gets greater. As things get more impossible they also get more obvious. As our needs get simpler, they get more unlikely to be fulfilled.

Duet For One

Tom Kempinski Samuel French, London 1981

Act 2

FELDMANN:

Don't play silly buggers with me, Miss Abrahams! I don't have the time for it, and I don't have the inclination! You think I just sit here dispensing pills and wisdom to keep my family in new dresses, well you're making a big mistake. We are engaged in a struggle here, Miss Madame; a struggle, yes. And you may pretend to yourself that you think that is very amusing and interesting and boring and sophisticated and other nonsense and rubbish, but that is not the case, and I would have kicked you and your money out long ago if it *were* the case. You think I am amused to hear you make flippant remarks about suicide and how many of my patients have killed themselves and other disgusting nonsense? You think because I sit here calmly and listen to all of it that I am just some kind of lay priest in the confessional box, here for your amusement or to unload the burden of your misfortune on to? Well you are totally and completely and stupidly *wrong*. For your cynical information, some of my patients *have* committed suicide. I have sat here and heard how the world and their families and society have destroyed them and made them unhappy beyond the ability of even a doctor to grasp. And then, because medical science and my skill were inadequate, I have received news of their deaths; by hanging, shooting, cutting their wrists in the bath, jumping from bridges, plunging rusty knives into their bellies. And sometimes their husbands or their wives or their children have come to me, and I have tried to explain, to comfort, to restore some hope. So this is not my prime area of comedy, you may possibly now understand. And, Miss Abrahams, may I also inform you that it is *I* who am bored by *your* displays of depression and cynicism and pretended unconcernedness, because they are just stupid and boring games, which hundreds

174

of patients have tried to get me to play with them, but which are simply symptoms of their unhappy condition, and so I resolutely refuse to play these games with them. Because, Miss Abrahams, Mrs Liebermann, the game here is a real one, a deadly ernest one, a life and death game, as a matter of fact. Let me give it to you straight, Madame, you are close to killing yourself. Yes. Very close. You are walking the fine line. And you think you know this, but the unconscious forces against which we struggle are actually pushing you far harder and closer than you are aware. And do you think I shall sit back and allow this enemy to triumph? No! We must give battle to these dark forces, and I do, and I am asking you, or rather I am *telling* you, Miss Abrahams, to add your weight to mine in this fight, and not to come in here with childish displays of your sordid giving in to this enemy, dragging yourself and your self-esteem into the dirt in front of me, because all I see is the slippery slope to despair, *and you will get off it, you hear me*!? [*Slight pause*] And you will resume with the medication I have prescribed immediately you leave here; is that clear!! Now cut it out, Miss Abrahams. Get off your arse, if I may use your terminology; get off your arse and fight!

Play With a Tiger

Doris Lessing

From *Plays of the '60s,*
Pan Books, London 1966

TOM:

You really do rub things in, Anna. All right then. For a number of years I've been seeing myself as a sort of a rolling stone, a fascinating free-lance, a man of infinite possibilities. It turns out that I'm just another good middle-class citizen after all – I'm comfort-loving, conventionally unconventional, I'm not even the Don Juan I thought I was. It turns out that I'm everything I dislike most. I owe this salutary discovery to you, Anna. Thank you very much.

Oh my God, you stupid little romantic. Yes, that's what you are, and a prig into the bargain. Very pleased with yourself because you won't soil your hands. Writing a little review here, a little article there, an odd poem or two, a reflection on the aspect of a sidelight on the backwash of some bloody movement or other – reading tuppenny-halfpenny novels for publishers, Mr Bloody Black's new book is or is not an advance on his last. Well, Anna, is it really worth it?

And worrying all the time how you're going to find the money for what your kid wants. Do you think he's going to thank you for living like this?

You live here, hand to mouth, never knowing what's going to happen next, surrounding yourself with bums and neurotics and failures. As far as you're concerned anyone who has succeeded at anything at all is corrupt. [*She says nothing*] Nothing to say, Anna? That's not like you.

176

Diner ★

Barry Levinson

From *Avalon/Tin Men/Diner,*
Faber & Faber, London 1990

SHREVIE:

Have you been playing my records?

Didn't I tell you the procedure? [*They have had this discussion before.*] They have to be in alphabetical order.

And what else?

They have to be filed according to year as well. Alphabetically and according to year.

And what else? [BETH *thinks.*] And what else?

Let me give you a hint. I found James Brown filed under the *J*'s instead of the *B*'s; but to top it off, you put him in the rock-and-roll section! Instead of the R-and-B section! How could you do that?!

Is it too much to keep records in a category? R and B with R and B. Rock and roll with rock and roll. You wouldn't put Charlie Parker with rock and roll, would you?

[BETH *says nothing.*]

Would you?!! [*exasperated*] *Jazz!! Jazz!! Jazz!!!!*

Don't you understand?! It's important to me! [*They stare at one another.* SHREVIE *is trying to control his temper.* BETH*'s eyes become watery.*]

Pick a record. Any record.

Pick a record!

[BETH *moves to the record rack and pulls out a record. She holds onto it, not sure what* SHREVIE *wants.*]

What's the hit side? [*She tells him – "Good Golly Miss Molly."*]

Ask me what's on the flip side?

Ask me what's on the flip side.

"Hey, Hey, Hey, Hey" – 1958 – Specialty Records. You never ask me what's on the flip side!

Every one of these means something. The label. The

producer. The year they were made. Who was copying whose style or expanding on it. I hear these, and they bring back certain times in my life.

[*He stares at her coldly.*]

Don't ever touch these again. Ever.

[*He starts out of the room. He turns back to* BETH.]

I first met you at Modell's sister's high-school graduation party. 1955. "Ain't That a Shame" was playing as I walked in the door.

[*He exits and slams the door shut.*]

When I Was a Girl I Used to Scream and Shout . . .

Sharman MacDonald   Faber & Faber, London 1990

Act 2 Scene 1

EWAN:

> [FIONA *creeps to the pool and gathers water in her hands. She moves over to* EWAN and drops water on him.]

> [*Screams*] Fucking bitch.

> [FIONA *moves away from him and sits staring out to sea.* EWAN *dries himself meticulously.*]

Jesus Christ, woman. What do you expect, creeping up on a man like that? Took my breath away. I mean, Jesus, Fiona. That water's freezing. It's not the bloody Mediterranean. What the hell do you have to play bloody stupid games for? I mean, shit, Fiona. Come on. What's a man supposed to do? I mean, shit, Fiona. Shit. [*Pause.*] Come here. Look at the bloody face on it. Come here. I forgive you. Come on, I'll give you a cuddle. Bloody hell, woman. Bloody listen, will you. Move your backside over here. I've said I forgive you. Jesus Christ, what do

178

you fucking well want? Dear God, woman, it's not as if I sodding well hit you. I mean, if I'd hit you you'd have something to bloody girn about. Don't be bloody ridiculous. [*Pause.*] You want me to say sorry to you. You sodding well do. You do. I sodding well won't. You've not a pissing hope. Shit. [*Pause.*] I'm fucking sorry. There. Is that bloody better?

    [FIONA *moves over to him.*]
Bloody smile then.

Events While Guarding the Bofors Gun

John McGrath   Plays and Players, 1966

O'ROURKE:

The Bofors gun, sirs, is a mighty fine thing. It is primarily a light anti-aircraft gun, designed – beautifully designed, you will agree – for the role of protecting infantry in the field and forward headquarters of all kinds from low-flying enemy aircraft. You may have observed what we call the magazine, into which we slip the little shells, four at a time. By Jove, sirs, when she fires one single shot, 'tis thunder, but when she challenges the straffing attacker on non-stop repeat, oho, sirs, she bucks and sweats and strains with joy, and delivers herself of thirty-two great little rounds per minute, belittling the thunder, and deafening the very welkin itself. You may have observed also, sirs, the two grand little seats, where the operators operate. One finds the height, his butty the angle, and do you know, sirs, that in the latest model of all, they say that one man does both, with the aid of electrical assistance. It is indeed a fine gun, the Bofors light ack-ack. It has been, of course, obsolete since 1942, the year it was put on the market, and even the ultimate in Bofors guns has no particular role to play in the event of a genuine war, with its nuclear fission. Even, need I say it, in the event of a more conventional conflict, it will be found to be very rarely in the same spot as the more mobile aircraft of today, and even if it were, they are too fast, and too small, to present a suitable target. It is an inefficient and obsolete weapon, sirs, of which our army has many thousands: and you have, in your wisdom, asked me, Gunner O'Rourke, to guard it with my life, thinking that as my thirtieth year looms up to strike me between the eyes, I would indeed do anything, anything, to preserve and shelter from all Bolshevik harm, a thing so beautifully useless, so poignantly past it, so wistfully outdated, as my youth, or a Bofors gun. I would, and shall, lay down my life for it. I have tried already, and failed. Here, in the sacred presence of the Bofors gun, I can only succeed.

Dylan

Sidney Michaels

Andre Deutsch, London 1964

DYLAN:

I'm me. I smoke too much. I drink too much. I never like to go to bed. But when I go to bed, I never like to have to get up! I sleep with women. I'm not much on men. Necrophilism – that's with dead bodies – leaves me cold. I never watch the clock and it doesn't pay much attention to me. I write poems and I read 'em out loud. I lie, I cry, I laugh, I cheat, I steal when I can. I must have an iron constitution as I've been abusing it for years to an extent which'd kill a good horse in a matter of hours. I love people, rich and poor people, dumb as well as smart people, people who like poetry and people who never heard of poetry.

I'm life's most devoted, most passionate, most shameless lover. I must be. And I like a good party and a good time and applause and lots of pats on my back and pots and hats full of jack which I then like to spend without stinting. Comforts make me comfortable; nails in my shoe, an ache in my tooth and grit in my eye do not. I have lived in a time when men have turned Jews into soap. I've been, I must tell you, ever since those days, a wee bit confused about the godly nature of the human creature. But I'm not as confused as anyone I ever met or heard of. Because I am me. And I know me. I've sung a few songs in thirty-nine years just for the pleasure of singing, but now I have come to a point in my life when I think I have something to say. I think it's something about having the guts to thumb your nose at the social shears that clip the wings of the human heart in our mushrooming, complex, cancerous age. I'm hot for fireworks in the dull of night. I want the factual, killing world should go back to fancy kissing for its livelihood. I'm about to write an opera with Stravinsky. A play on my own, my first, called *Under Milk Wood*. And I've been offered to play the lead in a play on Broadway. Things are looking up. But I'm spitting a lot of blood and blacking out more often than I'm used to, and I think I had a touch of the d.t.'s this past week as I've started seeing little things that aren't there – mice, for example. Miss Meg Stuart, my friend, suggested that I come to see you, Doctor, as it's entirely possible and not a little ironic, now that things are finally looking up – [*Long pause.*] that I'm dying.

Don Juan

Molière
Translated by Nicholas Enright   Currency, Sydney 1984

Scene 1

SGANARELLE:

Oh, Gusman, you poor fellow, believe me, you don't yet know the kind of man Don Juan is.

. . .And if you knew the fellow, you'd see it's a simple matter for him. I'm not saying he has changed his mind about Dona Elvira, I've got no proof of that – I left before him and he hasn't called for me since he arrived – but I will give you a few quiet words of warning. My master, Don Juan, is the greatest sinner the world has ever known. He's a madman, a dog, a devil, the Turk, a heretic, doesn't believe in Heaven, or Hell, or the Wolf-man, lives like a wild beast, a greedy hog, like Attila the Hun, shuts his ears to any criticism, and says all that you and I believe in is rubbish. You say he's married your mistress. If he felt strongly enough about her, he'd go further: he'd marry you as well, and her dog and her cat. It costs him nothing to make a marriage. It's his favourite trick to catch the beauties, and he's husband to the world. Married woman or unmarried, merchant class or peasant, there's nothing too hot or too cold for him. And if I told you the names of all the women he's married in various places, the list would last all day. You're surprised? You've gone pale! That's only an outline. I'd need a lot more brushwork to finish the portrait. Anyway, the wrath of Heaven will strike him down one day, and I'd rather be the Devil's man than his and he makes me see so many horrors I wish he was already . . . you-know-where. But a great-lord-bad-man is a terrible thing. I have to be loyal, despite what I know of him. It's fear that keeps me at it, stifles my feelings, forced me often to applaud the things that inside me I loathe. Here he is. We'd better part company. But listen to me. I told you all this in confidence, things just tumbled out of me. But if any of it gets back to him, I'll call you a liar.

Scene 2

DON JUAN:

What? You mean one should bind oneself forever to the first object of one's desire, give up the world for it, no longer have eyes for any other? A fine thing to take pride in the false honour of fidelity, to bury oneself eternally in one passion, to be dead from one's very youth to all the other beauties which may dazzle one's eyes! No, constancy is good only for fools. All beautiful women have the right to charm us, and she who has the advantage of being our first encounter should not strip the others of their just claim on our hearts. For my part, beauty delights me wherever I find it, and I yield easily to the gentle violence with which it captures us. There is no use my being engaged: the love I have for one lovely woman cannot engage my soul to do injustice to others. My eyes must always be ready to see quality in all women, and each of them receives from me the worship that nature demands of us. I cannot refuse my heart to anything I see is loveable. And when a beautiful face demands it of me, if I had ten thousand hearts I would give them all. The first stirring desire is unaccountably charming, and all the pleasure of love is in variety. One tastes such extraordinary sweetness in wearing down the heart of a young beauty with a hundred acts of devotion, in seeing one's delicate progress day by day, in breaking down the feeble resistance of a virgin soul with rages tears and sighs, in wearing away its little defences, conquering the scruples on which it prides itself, and then gently drawing it down whatever path one pleases. But as soon as one is the master, there's nothing more to say, nothing more to wish for. All the beauty of passion is gone, and we slumber until some new prize comes to awaken our desires, to arouse our hearts with the allure of a conquest yet to be made. In short, there is nothing so sweet as triumphing over a beautiful young creature's resistance, and in this cause I have the ambition of those conquerors who hurry ever onward from victory to victory, unable to restrain or limit their ambitions. There is nothing which can halt the march of my desires. I have within me a heart ready to love the whole world, and like Alexander the Great, I could wish for other worlds beyond this one, so that I could range further in the conquests of love.

Scene 4

DON LOUIS:

I can see that I embarrass you, and that you would happily be spared my visit. Truly, we are remarkably at odds you and I and if you are tired of seeing me, I am tired of your behaviour. Alas, we act in such ignorance when we will not let Heaven guide our destinies, but besiege it with our blind, thoughtless requests! I begged for a son with extraordinary fervour. My entreaties were unceasing. And the son I got by wearying Heaven with my prayers is the bugbear of my life, when he should be my joy and my consolation. Tell me, how do you think I should view your appalling record, this constant succession of sordid affairs, which besmirch my good name in the eyes of the King, exhausting his good will as I apologise for you? How despicable you are! Do you not blush to be so unworthy of your birth? Tell me, do you have any right to take pride in it? And what have you done in the world to earn the name gentleman? Do you think that the title and the crest are not enough, that we can glory in noble birth if our lives debase it? No, no, birth is nothing without virtue. We have no claim on our forebears' glory until we make ourselves in their image. Indeed, the reflected glory of their deeds binds us to reflect the same honour on them, to follow in their footsteps, to maintain their virtues if we are to be called their true heirs. But you are no scion of the stock that gave you birth. Your ancestors disown you. You have no part in their achievements. No, their fame is your dishonour, their glory a torch which lights your shame to the world. Finally, learn that a gentleman who lives an evil life is a monster in nature, that the first title of rank is virtue, that I esteem less the name that one signs than the deeds one does, and that the robber's son who is an honest man, I rank higher than a king's son who lives as you do.

. . . I can see my words touch your soul not at all. You are no son of mine, and your deeds have tested a father's love to its limit. Know that I will put a stop to your excesses sooner than you think, that you will feel my wrath before the wrath of Heaven, and that your punishment will cleanse me of the shame of being your father.

The Storm

Alexander Ostrovsky

Vintage Books, Random House, Canada 1961

KULIGIN:

[*comes out center stage, turning to the crowd*]. What are you afraid of, for heaven's sake, tell me! Every blade of grass now, every flower is enraptured, but we are hiding, we are afraid, as if of some disaster! The storm will kill us! This isn't a storm, but a blessing! Yes, a blessing! But everything is a storm for you! When the Northern Lights shine, you should enjoy them and marvel at the majesty: "Dawn arises from the midnight lands!" But you get terror-stricken and try to think whether it means war or plague. When a comet falls, I can't take my eyes off it! It's beautiful! You've got used to the stars, they're always the same, but this is something new; you should look and enjoy it! But you're frightened even to glance at the sky, and tremble all over. You've made everything into scarecrows for yourselves. What people! Look, I'm not afraid. Let's go!

The Comfort of Strangers

Harold Pinter Faber & Faber, London 1990

ROBERT:

My father was a very big man. All his life he wore a black moustache. When it turned grey he used a little brush to keep it black, such as ladies use for their eyes. Mascara.

Everybody was afraid of him. My mother, my four sisters. At the dining-table you could not speak unless spoken to first by my father. But he loved me. I was his favourite. He was a diplomat all his life. We spent years in London. Knightsbridge. Every morning he got out of bed at six o'clock and went to the bathroom to shave. No one was allowed out of bed until he had finished. My eldest sisters were fourteen and fifteen. I was ten. One weekend the house was empty for the whole afternoon. My sisters whispered together. Their names were Eva and Maria. Then they called me and they led me into my parents' bedroom. They told me to sit on the bed and be quiet. They went to my mother's dressing-table. They painted their fingernails they put creams and powder on their faces, they used lipstick, they pulled hairs from their eyebrows and brushed mascara on their lashes. They took off their white socks and put on my mother's silk stockings and panties. They sauntered about the room, looking over their shoulders into mirrors. They were beautiful women. They laughed and kissed each other. They stroked each other. They giggled with each other. I was enchanted. They fed my enchantment. It was a beautiful day. The sun began to set. They washed themselves, they put everything away, in its place, leaving no clue. They whispered to me that it was our secret, that we would keep it in our hearts for ever and never reveal it. But that night at dinner I felt my father staring at me, staring deep into me. He chewed, swallowed. He put his knife and fork

186

down, he looked at me. My heart started to beat, to thump, to beat, to thump. My father said, 'Tell me, Robert, what have you been doing this afternoon?' He knew. I knew he knew. He was God. He was testing me. And so I told him. I told him all that my sisters had done. I told him everything. My mother was silent. My sisters' faces were white. No one spoke. My father said, 'Thank you, Robert', and finished his dinner. After dinner my sisters and I were called to my father's study. They were beaten with a leather belt, without mercy. I watched this.

A month later they took their revenge.

ROBERT:

A month later they took their revenge. We children were again alone in the house. My youngest sisters, Alice and Lisa, came to me in the garden and said, 'Robert, Robert, come to the kitchen quickly. Eva and Maria have a treat for you.' I was suspicious but I went. I was so innocent. On the kitchen table were two big bottles of lemonade, a cream cake, two packets of cooking chocolate and a big box of marshmallows. And Maria said, 'Look, darling, this is all for you.' 'Why?' I asked. 'We want you to be kinder to us in future,' she said. 'When you have eaten all this you will remember how nice we are to you – and then you will be nice to us.' This seemed reasonable. 'But first,' Eva said, 'you must drink some medicine. This is very rich food and this medicine will protect your stomach and help you to enjoy it.' I was too greedy to question this. I drank the medicine – only slightly disgusting – and then I ate the chocolate and the cake and the marshmallows and drank a bottle of lemonade. And they applauded and said that only a *man* could drink a second bottle of lemonade, it would be beyond my capabilities, and I said, 'Give it to me,' and I drank the second bottle and I finished the chocolates and the marshmallows and the cake and they said, 'Bravo, bravo!' And then the kitchen began to spin round me and I badly needed to go to the lavatory and then suddenly Eva and Maria held me down and tied my hands together with a long piece of rope behind my back and Alice and Lisa were jumping up and down singing, 'Bravo, Robert!' And Eva and Maria dragged me across the corridor and hallway and into my father's study. They took the key from the inside, slammed the door and locked it. 'Bye, bye, Robert,' they called through the keyhole. 'Now you are big Papa in his study.'

I was locked in my revered, my feared father's study, where he received the diplomatic corps of London, the elite of the world. And I puked and pissed and shat all over my father's carpets and walls.

My father found me there. He said, 'Robert, have you been eating chocolate?' Then he nearly killed me. And then he didn't speak to me for six months.

I have never forgiven my sisters. My only solace was my mother. I grew so thirsty . . . at night. She brought me a glass of water every night and laid her hand upon my brow. She was so tender. When my father was away I slept in her bed. She was so warm, so tender.

But one afternoon the wife of the Canadian Ambassador was invited to tea. She brought her daughter, Caroline. When my mother showed her mother our garden – we were left alone, the children. Suddenly Eva said, 'Miss Caroline, do you sleep with your mother?' Caroline said, 'No. Do you?' And Eva said, '*He* does.' And all my sisters giggled and Caroline looked at me and smiled and said, 'I think that's really awfully sweet.'

[*He smiles.*]

And she became my wife. Not at that moment of course. We were both only eleven years old at the time.

Cyrano de Bergerac

Edmond Rostand

Translated by Anthony Burgess   Nick Hern Books, London

Act 3

CYRANO:

Shatter them all, these tokens –
Valentine hearts, arrows, the tinselled quiver,
Stale words, stale honey sipped in finicking drops
From tarnished gilded cups. What are they worth
Compared to the wild urge that shouts, that beckons
Our bodies to plunge and drown in the wild river?
               . . . In that most precious
Instant, I shall take all words that ever were,
Or weren't, or could, or couldn't be, and in
Mad armfuls, not bouquets, I'll smother you in them.
Oh god, how I love, I choke with love, I
Stumble in madness, tread a fiery region
Where reason is consumed, I love you beyond
The limits that love sets himself, I love,
I love. Your name, Roxane, swings like a brazen
Bell, telling itself – Roxane, Roxane –
In my heart's belfry, and I tremble –
Roxane, Roxane – with each bronze, gold,
Silver reverberation. Listen, I swing
Down the rope to earth's level, to each small thing
– Trivial, forgettable, unforgettable by me –
That ever you do or did. A year ago,
The twelfth of May it was, at noon's striking,
You left your house with your hair dressed a different way,
The former way not being to your liking,
And you know how, when you've been looking at the sun,
You see red suns everywhere, embossed
On everything, so that solar flood of your hair
Blinded me and bequeathed an after-image

189

Of heavenly goldness touching everything
With a royal touch.
                    . . . Love, the parasitic heavenly host,
A terribly jealous god has seized me with most
Wretched fury – and yet he seeks not to possess,
He's only mad to give. So my happiness
Is there to augment yours – even though
You forget, or never knew, the scourge of its flow.
I ask no more than to listen, twice, or thrice,
To the laughter born out of the sacrifice
Of mine. Each glance of your eyes begets some new
Virtue in me, new courage. Oh, can you
See this, feel it, understand? Do you sense
My heart rising towards you in this intense
Stillness, whose perfumed velvet wraps us close?
This night I speak, you listen. Never in my most
Reckless unreasonable dream have I hoped for this.
Now I can gladly die, knowing it is
My words that make you tremble in the blue
Shadow of the tree. For it is true –
You do tremble, like a leaf among the leaves,
Yes, and the passion of that trembling weaves
A spider filament that seeks me now,
Feeling its way along the jasmine bough.
                         . . . Ah, to die,
Death is all I need now after this
Summit gained.

Amadeus

Peter Shaffer

Penguin, London 1981

Act 1

SALIERI:

Capisco! I know my fate. Now for the first time, I feel my emptiness as Adam felt his nakedness . . .

[*Slowly he rises to his feet*]

Tonight at an inn somewhere in this city stands a giggling child who can put on paper, without actually setting down his billiard cue, casual notes which turn my most considered ones into lifeless scratches. *Grazie,* Signore! You gave me the desire to serve you – which most men do not have – then saw to it the service was shameful in the ears of the server. *Grazie!* You gave me the desire to praise you – which most do not feel – then made me mute. *Grazie tante!* You put into me perception of the Incomparable – which most men never know! – then ensured that I would know myself forever mediocre. [*His voice gains power*] *Why? What is my fault?*

. . . Until this day I have pursued virtue with rigour. I have laboured long hours to relieve my fellow men. I have worked and worked the talent you allowed me. [*Calling up*] *You know how hard I've worked!* – solely that in the end, in the practice of the art which alone makes the world comprehensible to me, I might hear Your Voice! And now I do hear it – and it says only one name: MOZART! . . . Spiteful, sniggering, conceited, infantine Mozart! – who has never worked one minute to help another man! – shit-talking Mozart with his botty-smacking wife! – *him* you have chosen to be your sole conduct! And *my* only reward – my sublime privilege – is to be the sole man alive in this time who shall clearly recognise your Incarnation! [*Savagely*] *Grazie e grazie ancora!*

[*Pause*]

So be it! From this time we are enemies, You and I! I'll not accept it from You – *Do you hear!* . . . They say God is not

191

mocked. I tell you, *Man* is not mocked! *I* am not mocked! . . . They say the spirit bloweth where it listeth: I tell you NO! It must list to virtue or not blow at all! [*Yelling*] *Dio Ingiusto!* You are the Enemy! I name Thee now – *Nemico Eterno!* And this I swear. To my last breath I shall *block* you on earth, as far as I am able!

[*He glares up at God. To audience*]

What use, after all, is Man, if not to teach God His lessons?

Five Finger Exercise

Peter Shaffer   Penguin, London 1972

Act 1 Scene 2

CLIVE:

All this stuff – right people, wrong people – people who matter. It's all so meaningless . . .

What can I say to them if they don't matter to me? Look, you just can't talk about people in that way. It's idiotic. As far as I'm concerned one of the few people who really matters to me in Cambridge is an Indian.

He's completely still. I don't mean he doesn't move – I mean that deep down inside him there's this happy stillness, that makes all our family rows and raised voices here like a kind of – blasphemy almost. That's why he matters – because he loves living so much. Because he understands birds and makes shadow puppets out of cardboard, and loves Ella Fitzgerald and Vivaldi, and Lewis Carroll; and because he plays chess like a devil and makes the best prawn curry in the world.

. . . These aren't my play-pals; they're important people. Important to me.

Important! It's important they should be alive. Every person they meet should be altered by them, or at least remember them with terrific – terrific excitement. That's an important person. Can't you understand?

[*Directly, his voice shaking with resentment.*] Has it ever occurred to you that *I* don't understand *you*? No. Of course not. Because you're the one who does the understanding around here – or rather fails to. [*Furiously.*] What work did you put in to being able to understand anybody?

D'you think it falls into your lap – some sort of a grace that enters you when you become a father?

You think you can treat me like a child – but you don't even know the right way to treat a child. Because a child is private and important and itself. Not an extension of you. Any more than I am. [*He falls quiet, dead quiet - as if explaining something very difficult. His speech slows and his face betrays an almost obsessed sincerity.*] I am myself. Myself. Myself. You think of me only as what I might become. What I might make of myself. But I am myself now - with every breath I take, every blink of the eyelash. The taste of a chestnut or a strawberry on my tongue is me. The smell of my skin is me, the trees and tables that I see with my own eyes are me. You should want to become me and see them as I see them, but we can never exchange. Feelings don't unite us, don't you see? They keep us apart. [*Rises and goes to sofa.*] And words are no good because they're unreal. We live away in our skins from minute to minute, feeling everything quite differently, and any one minute's just as true about us as any other. That's why a question like 'What are you going to be?' just doesn't mean anything at all - [*Sits during pause.*] Yes, I'm drunk. You make me drunk.

Rosencrantz and Guildenstern are Dead

Tom Stoppard   Faber & Faber, London 1967

PLAYER:

[*bursts out*] We can't look each other in the face! [*Pause, more in control.*] You don't understand the humiliation of it - to be tricked out of the single assumption which makes our existence viable - that somebody is *watching*. . . The plot was two corpses gone before we caught sight of ourselves, stripped naked in the middle of nowhere and pouring ourselves down a bottomless well.

There we were - demented children mincing about in clothes that no one ever wore, speaking as no man ever spoke, swearing love in wigs and rhymed couplets, killing each other with wooden swords, hollow protestations of faith hurled after empty promises of vengeance - and every gesture, every pose, vanishing into the thin unpopulated air. We ransomed our dignity to the clouds, and the uncomprehending birds listened. [*He rounds on them.*] Don't you see?! We're *actors* - we're the opposite of people! Think, in your head, *now*, think of the most . . .*private* . . . secret . . . *intimate* thing you have ever done secure in the knowledge of its privacy . . . [*He gives them - and the audience - a good pause.*] Are you thinking of it? *Well, I saw you do it!*

We're actors . . . We pledged our identities, secure in the conventions of our trade; that someone would be watching. And then, gradually, no one was. We were caught, high and dry. It was not until the murderer's long soliloquy that we were able to look around; frozen as we were in profile, our eyes searched you out, first confidently, then hesitantly, then desperately as each patch of turf, each log, every exposed corner in every direction proved uninhabited, and all the while the murderous King addressed the horizon with his dreary interminable guilt . . . Our heads began to move, wary as lizards, the corpse of unsullied Rosalinda peeped through his fingers, and the King faltered. Even then, habit and a stubborn trust that our audience spied upon us from behind the nearest bush, forced our bodies to blunder on long after they had emptied of meaning, until like runaway carts they dragged to a halt. No one came forward. No one shouted at us. The silence was unbreakable, it imposed itself upon us; it was obscene. We took off our crowns and swords and cloth of gold and moved silent on the road to Elsinore.

Lovers and Other Strangers

Renee Taylor and
Joseph Bologna Ashley Famous Agency, New York 1968

MIKE:

I'm not getting married!. . . . I said, "I'm not getting married!" I told you this would happen!. . . . I told you I wasn't ready. Do you remember, I said, "Susan, if I ask you to marry me, can I take it back if I want too?" And you said I could, didn't you?. . . Well, I'm taking it back now. I mean it's not that I don't love you, because I love you. I really love you, Susan, but it just can't be for keeps. I tried Susan, I really tried, but it's getting close. There's only four days left. Just four more days and I can't go any further . . . No, sir. No, Ma'am. Uh-uh. No chance. No, siree . . . Uh-uh. That's it. I can't do it. That's it!

Please stop looking at me like that. You shouldn't take it personally. It's nothing against you. It's the times we live in. India's overpopulated! We'll all be sterilized soon. The suicide rate is up. The air is polluted. Is that the kind of world you want to get married in? Is it, Susan? Is it?. . . I know what you're trying to do – make me look like the bad one. Well, it won't work. It won't work. Because I'm clean. I'm clean. You knew exactly what you were doing. You knew I was a confirmed bachelor. You knew I had trouble getting involved, but that didn't stop you. No, not you, baby. You decided to marry me and that was it. Well, who do you think you are, playing God with another person's life. Well, I have no pity for you. None whatsoever, because you're getting just what you deserve. So, get off my back. I owe you nothing, baby. Get it? I owe you nothing!. . .

All right, Susan. I've got to put my cards on the table. I didn't want to tell you this because I didn't want to hurt your feelings. You're just not my dream girl. I'm sorry. I wish you were, but

197

let's face it, Susan. My heart doesn't beat fast when you come into a room. I don't get goose pimples when I touch you. I'm just not nervous when I'm with you. You're too vulnerable. You're too human. You've got too many problems. And, Susan, there's something about you that really bothers me. Maybe it wouldn't be important to another guy, but I think about it a lot. Susan, you have very thin arms.

So, I don't think I could be faithful. I mean, I want to be faithful, but I just don't think I can. Ever since we got engaged, I walk down the street and I want to grab every ass I see. That's not normal. If you were my dream girl, I'd never give other women a second thought. Don't you understand, I need somebody more perfect, then it wouldn't be so much work for me to love and be faithful. I could just show up.

Look, you'll get over me. After a while, you'll find another boy. Just promise me you won't sleep with anyone until you get married. Will you promise me that, Susan? Will you? . . .

That's it. It's all over.

[HE *picks up her hand and shakes it*]

Goodbye. I'm sorry. That's it.

On the Eve

Ivan Turgenev   Penguin, London 1950

SHUBIN:

I'll tell you the cause of all this, Andrei Petrovich. What you have been describing are the sensations of a lonely individual who doesn't really live, but simply looks on and is overcome by his feelings. What's the good of *looking*? Live, and be a man. No matter how often you knock at Nature's door, she won't answer in words you can understand – for Nature is dumb. She'll vibrate and moan like a violin string, but you mustn't expect a song. A living soul, *that* will respond to you – above all a woman's soul. And so, my dear sir, I recommend you to get yourself a soul mate, then all your melancholy sensations will vanish. That is what we 'need', to use your own word. You see, this restlessness, this sadness – it's really just a sort of hunger. Give your belly the right stuff to eat, and everything will straighten itself out. Take your place in space as a physical body, my friend. And this 'Nature', what is it, what's it for? Listen for yourself: Love . . . what a warm strong word! Nature . . . how cold and pedantic. Therefore I say 'Here's to Marya Petrovna' . . . or maybe not her . . . not Marya Petrovna, it really doesn't matter! You know what I mean.

. . . If you fall in love, then you can't go wrong. . . . Nature affects us in that way because it awakens the need for love, but is not capable of satisfying it. It drives us gently into other, living arms, but we don't realize this, and expect something from Nature herself. Oh, Andrei, Andrei, how lovely this sunshine is, and that sky too, everything, everything around us is lovely, and yet you're grieving. But if at this moment you were holding the hand of a woman you loved, if that hand and all of her were yours, if you even saw with her eyes and felt, not with your own lonely feelings, but with hers – then, Andrei, it wouldn't be grief and anxiety that Nature stirred up in you, you wouldn't stop to

199

contemplate its beauty; no, you'd find Nature itself would exult and sing, it would echo your own rhapsodies – because you would have given to Nature, dumb Nature, a tongue.

SHUBIN:

Yes, it's youth and glory and courage. It's life and death, struggle, defeat and triumph, love, liberty and fatherland! How fine, how fine! God grant everyone as much! That's not like sitting up to your neck in a bog and taking up an attitude of brave indifference, when in point of fact you don't care anyway. With them, it's a case of keying themselves up to play to the whole world, or perish!

Yes, Insarov is worthy of her. And yet what nonsense that is! Nobody's worthy of her. Insarov . . . Insarov . . . What's the point of all this false modesty? Let's admit he's got courage and knows how to stand up for himself – up to now he's not achieved any more than we poor sinners, so are we really such wash-outs? Well, take me, am I such a wash-out, Uvar Ivanovich? Has God been altogether unkind to me? Hasn't he given me any ability or talent? Who knows, maybe Pavel Shubin will be a famous name in time to come. Look at that half-penny of yours on the table there: perhaps a hundred years hence that bit of copper will go towards a statue erected in honour of Pavel Shubin by a grateful posterity!

O great philosopher of the Russian soil! Every word you utter is pure gold: it shouldn't be me that they put up a statue for, but you – and I'll take on the job myself! Just as you're lying there, in that very pose – so that you can't say whether there's more power or laziness in it – that's how I'll do it! How justly you struck at my egoism and self-esteem. You're right, you're right: it's no good bragging and talking about oneself. We haven't got anyone among us, no real people, wherever you look. It's all either minnows and mice and little Hamlets feeding on themselves in ignorance and dark obscurity, or braggarts throwing their weight about, wasting time and breath and blowing their own trumpets. Or else there's the other kind, always studying themselves in disgusting detail, feeling their pulses with every sensation that they experience and then reporting to themselves: 'That's how I feel, and that's what I think.' What a useful, sensible sort of occupation. No, if we'd had some proper people among us, that girl, that sensitive spirit, wouldn't have left us, she wouldn't have slipped out of our hands like a fish into the water. Why is it, Uvar Ivanovich? When is our time coming? When are we going to produce some real people?

Pack of Lies

Hugh Whitemore   Amber Lane, London 1983

Act 2

BOB:

As it happened, the war wasn't as bad for us as it was for most people; my job was a reserved occupation, you see, I was working on aircraft fuel systems, so at least I know I wouldn't be called up, at least I knew we wouldn't be separated. Even so there was the blitz, God that was bad enough, I mean every time there was a raid, every time I heard those damn sirens, my stomach would turn over, God I can feel it now, that terrible lurch inside – and all the time wondering would I get home and find nothing there, just bricks and rafters and broken glass, everything gone, Barbara gone, everything just . . . well, it doesn't bear thinking about. I used to rush back to Cranley Drive just as fast as I could, praying like mad, which was daft because I've never been a believer, never, but I suppose everyone's the same, aren't they, I mean at times like that what else can you do? [*Pause.*] It's always frightened me, always, the thought of losing her, of being alone. I used to have nightmares

201

about it. But then I'd think – Come on, don't be such a chump, there's no point in getting morbid about these things; you're three years older than her and men usually die first anyway, so you'll always have Barbara, there's nothing to worry about, you'll always have her.

Act 2

PETER:

In the winter of 1932, when the Depression was at its worst, a friend took me to a meeting – an informal and private meeting – in New York City. On our way there we walked along Riverside Drive. Scores of unemployed men were camping there in tiny shacks and shanties. I saw in their faces a degree of hopelessness and despair I had never seen before. [*Brief pause.*] I remembered those brave words about 'life, liberty and the pursuit of happiness.' And I felt a great surge of anger that such noble ideals should have been so betrayed – forgotten. Why did it happen – how? [*Brief pause.*] When I got to the meeting, I found a small group of maybe seven or eight men and women, mostly young, mostly about my age, all talking politics. It was cold that night, and there was no heat in the apartment; we stood around wearing overcoats. An older man read to us from the works of Marx and Lenin. His voice was soft, almost gentle; I've never forgotten it. He said: 'The ruin of capitalism is imminent. Every attempt to establish a truly human society upon the old capitalist foundations is foredoomed to absolute failure. We are thus confronted by two alternatives, and two only. There must be either complete disintegration, further brutalization and disorder; absolute chaos, or else Communism.' [*Brief pause.*] That evening my whole life changed.

My Brother's Keeper

Nigel Williams   Faber & Faber, London 1985

SAM:

When you breathe life into things, Tony, it's always your life.
Not their life. They want to feel a bit free. They don't want you
telling them they're free.

  Oh, you always had such life. As a little kid you had such *life* in
you. I can remember when you were born. Going to the hospital
to see you. I was nearly 10. Christ. Nearly 10. An old man. And
there was you like a little red rat. Screaming and punching and
just . . . well . . . just *alive*. And you never stopped being alive.
You never stopped waddling up to people and looking up into
their faces and letting them know how bloody alive you were.
[*Pause.*] But it was just you, Tony. It wasn't the other buggers. It
was just you. It was just you having this good time. You had this
life. And you carried it around like a candle flame and you hoped
it would set light to the grass and the trees and the buildings and
the streets until all of England was blazing with this light of
yours. You called it all sorts of names but *all* it was, in the end,
was this life of yours. And it'll set light to nothing, Tony. Not in
the big wide world outside not here not even in fucking Finland.
Because while you've been carrying this life of yours so carefully
in your hands people have been dying and failing and going
dark. All round you. Everywhere. [*Pause.*] He is going to die,
Tony.

TONY:

I don't know what to do, Sammy. I've run out of things. I can't
get my act together. Even talking. You see? Even the sacred
bloody play-acting he and I always went for. No good. [*Showing
his fear and despair for the first time*] I've been up every day this

week and I've pulled out all the old stops. Done the lot, you know? Will to live. Jesus, she doesn't know the half of it. I've run through all his great performances. I've done him doing Lear, I've done me watching him do Lear, I've done – [*Desperate*] There's nothing more I can say. I can feel it in the room. I can feel death in the room. I've done my act and still it won't go away. It's sitting on that bed there, looking across at him, grinning and feeling the edge of its razor. And all of the things I've thought were beautiful or clever or important about life. They won't help it to go away. It doesn't care you see. I tell it I'm a Labour Party supporter. I tell it I'm against Cruise. I tell it I'm a family man. I tell it I was the Most Promising Playwright of 1973. But it doesn't want to know, Sammy. It sits there on that bed turning over that old cut-throat razor, just like the one he had in the bathroom, remember? And it won't go away. I've told it I'm sorry for being conceited and loud-mouthed and insensitive. I've apologized for tormenting a boy called Forster in form 3A at a public school in North London in 1964. But death isn't interested. I'm scared, Sammy. That's how things are with me at the moment. I am absolutely fucking terrified.

Will you take care of it? Is that it? Do I wind up running round the ward after you shouting 'Sammee – Sammee' like when we were kids, is that it? Will you think of something? You were great when my rabbit died, I remember. I seem to remember you telling me it had gone to heaven. Very forcefully.

I'm afraid of other people dying. I want to go first. Before everyone else. I don't want to be upstaged.

TONY:

It's got to be gone through, Samuel. Look at him. I know what's been happening. She's never tried. She's gone through the motions. But she's never actually tried. And until she does he's going to go on, retreating, an inch at a time, further away from the light. The way he retreated all his bloody life. Because she let him. Because she wouldn't love him enough. Don't you see that? And I tell you this – it isn't a piece of whimsy, it's hard fact, Samuel. If you don't love people they die.

I'm going to get her, Sammy. I'm going to make her bloody talk to him. Not the way she always did. Like he was some troublesome piece of furniture. But as if he was a person. Understand that? The will to live. The will to live for what?

They don't want to live. They want to die. They want their real feelings to wither like leaves on a tree. They want out. They want to avoid the issue. They want to say anything but what is in their hearts. But they mustn't be allowed to. They've got to say what they feel and whether they love or whether they hate and they've got to be bloody made to see that life is too precious to be allowed to slip away.

TONY:

'For me.' 'Do it for me.' That's what they say to children, isn't it? She used to say it to me. 'For me.' Every mouthful part of a psychological war. Well, don't do it for me, Dad. Do it for yourself. [*Holding out plate*] There it is. British Hospital Food. If you can eat that you can eat anything. It's a challenge. Go on. It won't be here for ever, you know. The way things are going in the National Health they won't be able to afford food soon. [*Quiet*] Eat it for yourself, Dad. Eat it for yourself. You will get better. But you must want to. The will. Remember that old thing? [*Pause.*] Just a mouthful, Pater. Just a mouthful. One mouthful. Then – who knows? Just one. Then you'll be off and away. It's been three days, Dad. Please. They'll put you on a – [*Pause.*] Look. Just a crumb. A symbolic act. Holy Communion. Take this in remembrance of me. Just a crumb. [*Desperate*] COME ON!

[*Pause.*] I am staying here until I see that plate empty. I am going to be standing over you until I see a clean plate. Do you want chocolates? Well, if you don't have quiche you don't have chocolates. What's that? You don't want chocoates? That's cheating. Don't you want to grow up healthy and strong like the other boys? Don't you want to get married? Shame on you. You want to die? [*Close*] Listen – dying's awful. Dying's climbing into a black plastic bag and zipping it up over your head. Don't give me that resurrection and the life bit because I don't believe a word of it.

I like you fine as it happens. I don't fancy going to your funeral. I mean, you won't be there, will you? I just don't want you to die, you understand?

Please. Eat the fucking thing. Please.

I'm getting cross now. I am getting really angry. Before I was just pretending to be cross but now I really am. Cross. Really cross.

EAT IT! EAT IT, DAMN YOU! EAT IT! People have blessed the plain with the golden grain to get this made up for you. Packers have packed. Bakers have baked. Eat it. Stand up for your stomach. Stand up for yourself, against them. The way you didn't that afternoon in our front hall twenty-five years ago as she said, 'I'm going out' and you said, 'Don't leave me' and she said 'I'm going out' and your lower lip trembled and you started to cry, I've never forgotten it, Dad, never. I was on your side, Daddy. I still am. Get up. Please. Be like I wanted you to be then. Laying waste to all around you. For me. Please. EAT THE FUCKING THING!

GET IT DOWN YOU!

DON'T TURN YOUR HEAD AWAY! DON'T BACK AWAY FROM IT! ALL YOUR LIFE YOU WALKED AWAY FROM LIVING! YOU LET THEM WALK ALL OVER YOU, DAD! PLEASE DON'T TURN YOUR HEAD AWAY!

The American Dream

Edward Albee   Samuel French, New York 1961

YOUNG MAN:

We were identical twins - he and I - not fraternal - identical; we were derived from the same ovum; and in *this*, in that we were twins not from separate ova but from the same one, we had a kinship such as you cannot imagine. We - we felt each other breathe - his heartbeats thundered in my temples - mine in his - our stomachs ached and we cried for feeding at the same time . . . But we were separated when we were still very young, my brother, my twin and I - inasmuch as you can separate one being. We were torn apart - thrown to opposite ends of the continent. I don't know what became of my brother - to the rest of myself - except that from time to time, in the years that have passed, I have suffered losses - that I can't explain. A fall from grace - a departure of innocence - loss - loss. How can I put it to you? All right; like this: once - it was as if all at once my heart became numb - almost as though I - almost as though - just like that - it had been wrenched from my body - and from that time I have been unable to love. Once - I was asleep at the time - I awoke, and my eyes were burning. And since that time I have been unable to see anything, *anything*, with pity, with affection - with anything but - cool disinterest. And my body - even there - since one time - one specific agony - since then I have not been able to love anyone with my body. And even my hands - I cannot touch another person and feel love. And there is more - there are more losses, but it all comes down to this: I no longer have the capacity to feel anything. I have no emotions. I have been drained, torn asunder - disembowelled. I have, now, only my person – my body, my face. I use what I have – I let people love me – I accept the syntax around me, for while I know I cannot relate – I know I must be related *to*. I let people love me – I let people touch me – I let them draw pleasure from my body – from my presence – from the fact of me – but that is all it comes to. As I told you, I am incomplete – I can feel nothing. I can feel nothing. And so – here I am – as you see me. I am – but this – what you see. And it will always be thus.

The Lady and the Clarinet

Michael Cristofer Dramatists Play Service, New York 1985

JACK:

Well, I did it. It's done. Finished. I finished it. I did it. Jesus. I can't believe it. Can you believe it? Just now. Really. What, ten, fifteen minutes ago. Maybe twenty. Twenty-five at the outside. I'm still shaking. Look at me. God. I feel great. I feel like a new person. I've been thinking about you every day. Every word you said ringing in my ears. You were right, you know? You were right about all of it. I knew you were right. But I didn't know what to do about it. No. I knew what to do but I didn't know *how* to do it. No. I knew how. But I couldn't. At least I didn't think I could. But I could. I did. I did it. We were sitting on the sofa. The kids were asleep. We were watching the TV. And one of my commercials came on. The one with the man swimming around in the toilet, you know. And I turned to her, I turned to Marge and I said, that's me. And she said, yeah, I know, I remember when you made it. And I said, no, I don't mean the commercial, I mean, that man, that man in the toilet, that's me. She just looked at me for a minute, and then she said, yeah. I have to get out, I said. And she said, yeah, you better, before you get pissed on. And then she laughed. She laughed so hard that I started laughing, too. And then she said – she was still laughing – what are you going to do? And I said – and I was still laughing, too – I said, I think we should separate. And we kept laughing. We haven't had a good laugh for years. We were laughing so hard we were crying. And she said, yeah, maybe we better separate. Then she kissed me and we started fooling around. The way she looked, she was smiling, laughing, she was beautiful. You should have seen her. I got so turned on, I jumped on her, it was incredible, the best it's ever been. And then, after, we went upstairs, she helped me pack. I picked up the suitcases, kissed her good-bye and here I am.

[*Luba hands a glass of wine to Jack. He tosses down the glasss of wine, puts glass on table.*]

Thanks.

Home Front

James Duff   Dramatists Play Service, New York 1985

JEREMY:

I trusted you once because you were my father but now I know things. I can see how things are. I've been somewhere – you know what you did? You sent me someplace where they didn't fight for anything but to stay alive. I've – I've seen things – things that scared me so bad I can't remember them. It won't ever go away. So fuck you and that crap about honor, mister. It was your honor, mister, don't you know that. I'm not embarrassing. I'm the embarrassment. Just my being here embarrasses you. 'Look at what I did to my own son.' That's what it says, my being here. O.K. Look up. Look up. LOOK UP! Do you recognise me, mister? I'm the shame you've been living with for the past year. I'm the shame you can't get rid of. A Viet Cong. A gook. G-O-O-K. There, I spelled it out for you. Anyway, I could hardly move. And I kept thinking this it it. I'm dead. It's over. Why? And we spent the rest of the day on the hill. And it started to get dark and then out of the blue this white thing started waving. And this gook stands up and kaboom, the sergeant shoots him. Not bad. But it – it hurt him. And we all ran up. Carefully. And there he was at the top. By himself. Just him. No more grenades, no more bullets. Just him. And the sergeant, he turned to me and he said kill him. And I said, he's a prisoner, and the sergeant said we bury prisoners in Viet Nam, soldier. And I – I – put the – the gun to my shoulder and I looked at the gook on the ground and he – he started screaming, ninety-to-nothing. And even though I didn't know the words, I understood everything he was saying. Don't do it. Don't kill me. And – I – I – the sergeant said, that's an order, soldier, and this is how we take prisoners in 'Nam, soldier, and the guy just kept crying and begging and the sergeant said, did you hear me, that's an order and I tried to pull the trigger, and I . . . his face. It started – it started changing. And I thought – it started to change, right in front of me. And this guy got up on his knees and it was you. All along it was you. You killed those people. With your fucking duty and your fucking embarrassment. And I blew your fucking brains out all over the top of that hill. I killed you. I killed you over and over again just to survive, man, I killed you everywhere I could find you. And here I am, I get home, and here I am and you're still here. Here you still are. Kicking me out of my own house with a couple of thousand bucks and a word about what is right for me to do. I killed those peole over there for nothing. It was for nothing. Nothing. Nothing. All the time I thought I was doing it, it was only you I wanted.

[*He brings the gun up level to his father's chest and pulls the trigger. There is the sound of a click.*]
It was you.

Beyond Therapy

Chris Durang

Samuel French, New York 1983

Act 2

BRUCE:

You're upset about Bob, aren't you? Bob will get used to the idea of us, I just tried to make it happen too soon. He's innately very flexible. Will you marry me?

Prudence, I believe one should just *act* – without thought, without reason, act on instinct. Look at the natives in Samoa, look at Margaret Mead. Did they think about what they were doing? Think of people who become heroes during emergencies and terrible disasters – they don't stop to fret and pick things apart, they just *move*, on sheer adrenalin. Why don't we think of our lives as some sort of uncontrollable disaster, like *The Towering Inferno* or *Tora! Tora! Tora!* and then why don't we just *act* on instinct and adrenalin. I mean, put that way, doesn't that make you just want to go out and get married?

I don't want lots and lots of people – I want you, and children, and occasionally Bob. Is that so bad? Aren't you afraid of being lonely? And aren't all your girlfriends from college married by now? And you know you should really have children *now*, particularly if you may want more than one. I mean, soon you'll be at the end of your child-bearing years. I don't mean to be mean bringing that up, but it is a reality. I mean time is running out for you. And me too. We're not twenty anymore. Do you remember how old thirty used to seem? . . .

These are realities, Prudence. I may be your last chance, maybe no one else will want to marry you until you're forty. And it's hard to meet people. You already said that Shaun Cassidy was too young. I mean, we have so little time left to ourselves, we've got to grab it before it's gone.

Prudence, I think you and I can make each other happy.

211

Boy's Life

Howard Korder

Grove, New York 1989

Scene 6

PHIL:

I would have destroyed myself for this woman. Gladly. I would have eaten garbage. I would have sliced my *wrists* open. Under the right circumstances, I mean, if she said, "Hey, Phil, why don't you just cut your wrists open," well, come on, but if *seriously*. . . We clicked, we connected on so many things, right off the bat, we talked about God for *three hours* once, I don't know what good it did, but that *intensity* . . . and the first time we went to bed, I didn't even touch her. I didn't *want* to, understand what I'm saying? And you know, I played it very casually, because, all right, I've had some rough experiences, I'm the first to admit, but after a couple of weeks I could feel we were right there, so I laid it down, everything I wanted to tell her, and . . . and she says to me . . . she says . . . "Nobody should ever need another person that badly." Do you *believe* that? "Nobody should ever . . ."! What is that? Is that something you saw on TV? I dump my *heart* on the table, you give me Joyce Dr. Fucking Brothers? "Need, need," I'm saying I *love* you, is that wrong? Is that not allowed anymore?

[*Pause*]

And so what if I did need her? Is that so bad? All right, crucify me, I needed her! So *what*! I don't want to be by myself, when I'm by myself I feel like I'm going out of my mind, I do. I sit there, I'm thinking forget it, I'm not gonna make it through the next *ten seconds*, I just can't *stand* it. But I do, somehow, I get through the ten seconds, but then I have to do it all over again, 'cause they just keep coming, all these . . . seconds, floating by, while I'm waiting for something to happen, I don't know what, a car wreck, a nuclear war or something, that sounds awful but at least there'd be this *instant* when I'd know I was alive. Just once. 'Cause I look in the mirror, and I can't believe I'm really there. I

212

can't believe that's me. It's like my body, right, is the size of, what, the Statue of Liberty, and I'm inside it, I'm down in one of the legs, this gigantic hairy leg, I'm scraping around inside my own foot like some tiny fetus. And I don't know who I am, or where I'm going. And I wish I'd never been born. [*Pause.*] Plus, my hair is falling out, that really *sucks*.

Nobody

Howard Korder   Grove, New York 1989

MAN:

In October of 1879, Mr. J.P. Morgan sat down at a table with the Jew Baron Rothschild in the city of Vienna, Europe. This is documented. In front of them was a globe of the planet called Earth. They took a cake knife and sawed it straight down the middle. You want to hear some more.

The Bolshevik Revolution was designed and paid for by the Bank of New York. Fact. Franklin Theodore Roosevelt, he was a great man? In 1934 the International Monetary Fund guaranteed him a crown for prolonging the depression until Japan could mobilize. Here is a surprise. Adolf Hitler, a puppet of the Zionist-Banker Conspiracy, hired to fake the extermination of the Jews. Shot dead in the bunker before he could talk. "What does this got to do with me." This country, the United States we live in, will go bankrupt in 1994, according to a plan drawn up one hundred years ago. Computer simulations in Tel Aviv, Israel for turning New York, Chicago, Los Angeles into death camps. There is literature available on this subject. You understand what's going on now?

All this is ending. The world you know. What happened to the farmers, that's just the start. Forces are ruling our lives. We kick ourselves for fucking up the whole time they're rolling us to the furnace in a boxcar. In December of 1987 I was dismissed from my position at Shale Technologies without explanation. Since that time it has been made impossible for me to hold a job. You ever fire a gun into a living human person?

Well, you may have to, my friend. If you care about this way of life, you may very well have to. [*Pause.*] Every Thursday at seven-thirty there is a meeting in the Union Hall on Seneca Avenue. I think you need to show up.

The Fisher King

Richard Lagravenese
Applause, New York 1991

JACK:

Hi! . . . It's Jack . . . How are you doing! . . . you look good . . . You do . . . Hey . . . You gonna wake up for me? Huh? . . . This isn't over, is it? . . . You think you're going to make me do this, don't you? . . .

[*sternly*] Well, forget it! No fucking way! . . . I don't feel responsible for you, or for any of them! Everybody has bad things happen to them . . . I'm not God. I don't decide . . . People survive.

[*pause*]

Say something!? . . . Everything's been going great! Great! I'm . . . I'm gonna have my own cable talk show, with an incredible equity I might add . . . I . . . I . . . have an . . . an incredibly gorgeous fucking girlfriend . . . I . . . I am living an *incredible fucking life!!!* . . . So don't lay there in your comfortable little coma and think I'm about to risk all of that because I feel responsible for you!

[*to the other* PATIENTS]

214

I am not responsible!
[*to* PARRY]
And I don't feel guilty . . . You've got it easy.

[*intensely*] I'm out there every day. Every day trying to figure out what the hell I'm doing . . . why, no matter what I have, it feels like I have nothing . . . So don't think I feel sorry for you! It's easy being nuts! Try being me! . . .

[*beat*]
So I won't do this. I do not believe in this. And don't give me that stuff about *being the one! There is nothing . . . nothing special about me!* I control my own destiny - not some overweight fairies. I say what I'm going to do and *I am not risking my life to get some fucking cup for some fucking vegetable. . .* And even if I did do this, I want you to know it wouldn't be because I had to! It wouldn't be 'cause I feel guilty or cursed or . . . or . . . bad or responsible or anything . . . shit . . . If I do this . . . and I mean If! . . . It's because I want to do this . . . for you. That's all!! For you!

[*(he kisses* PARRY's *forehead*]
Don't go anywhere . . . huh?

The Sex Organ

John Quincy Long

TED:
O.K.
O.K.
What's the product?
Budweiser
Budweiser beer
good beer
terrific beer
beers beer
drinkers beer
drink drink
drunk drink
drink of drinks
drink of drunks
Kinky drink
Gamey drink
The game drink
Drink at the game
Drink with the boys at the game
Game
Game
Sport
The drink of sports
Sporting life
Boy's life
Life in prison
Homicide
Murder
Murder plot
Abattoire
Abbot

Abbott
and Costello?
No
Abbot
Abbot
About
A boot
Das Boot
Boot!
Couldn't pour piss out of a boot

That's it
Fishing
The guys
Fishing
Hip boots
You know
Waders
Big rubber boots
Our guy is showing the other guys his waders
New waders his wife just bought him
Flexing suspenders
Tromping around
Into the river at last
Sighs of pleasure
Whoops
There's a leak
No there isn't
The guys
The buddies
They've snuck up and filled his waders with water
With a hose
With a bucket full of minnows
No
I got it
I got it
The guy
Our guy

He gets these boots as a Christmas present
Right?
From his son daughter wife mother father grandfather
Whatever
Shots of the family under the tree
Shots of whoever handing Dad his lumpengift
What could it be?
Surprise
Waders
Cute
He fantasizes himself to the river with his buddies
Budweiser in hand
No
No
Better yet
Much better
He's cleaning out . . .
The other's too complicated
He's cleaning out the closet
No
The garage
Yeah
The garage
Cleaning out the garage by himself
Oh tedium
What a drag
Finds the waders
By himself in the garage he finds the waders
He puts them on feeling deliciously silly
Fantasy
Fantasy
He's at the river
He can almost see it
We can almost see it
Maybe we do see it
I don't know
He's casting
The trout are nibbling

MacNibbles?
No
Then
His buddies are there
Horsing around
À la loo
À la loo
Fun fun fun
Drink drink drink
Then sonofabitch
His buddies are there
They really are
Peeking in through the dirty garage window
Watching him
Laughing
Friends
Friendly friends
Looking through the window
Sweatshirts
Baseball caps askew
Then
Payoff
They hold up . . .
The Bud
Ho
God
Whatafuckinconcept

The Incredibly Famous Willy Rivers

Stephen Metcalfe

American Theatre, Vol 2, No. 10, London 1986

Scene 2

PRISONER:

I have watched you play so many times . . .

In my opinion, you're an artist. You always have been. Like me.

An artist changes one's perception of reality. I changed yours a lot.

Don't thank me. At the time, changing your perception of reality wasn't my intention.

I was trying to kill you. [*Pause*] However, since death might be considered a drastic change in perception, I guess you could say my intentions have been consistent from the beginning. Artistically speaking.

. . .

You ever killed anybody?

Ever want to? I bet you have. It's great. You're so in control. Of course I'm talking premeditated. You're so powerful. You walk down the street and no one knows how powerful you are. You're like God. All you have to do is act and everything changes. You've taken a color out of a painting and substituted one of your own. You've given somebody else's melody different notes. You're a pebble that's been dropped in a pond. Concentric circles get wider and wider . . .

Why you?

You look good. People like you. Girls, I bet, like you. I bet they want to fuck you. I bet you have fun. I don't have fun. I never did. Why you. Why not me. Why not me!?

I was contemplating the President but it didn't look like he'd be passing through town for quite some time. You were elected.

. . .

If you must know, it was nothing personal. When I pulled the trigger I wasn't even thinking of you. No. I was thinking of me. I was thinking of me and what everybody else was gonna be thinking of me.

. . .

I have gotten over a hundred death threats! And at least twenty-five proposals of marriage. That's something.

There's a campaign started to free me.

Oh! And I've found Jesus.

. . .

Before we met? I was a custodial engineer. I worked at a hotel. I picked up after people like you. Televisions thrown from the fourteenth floor in an attempt to hit the swimming pool. Parties. Groupies. I heard of this one girl, she was casting molds of you people? Of your . . . things. For posterity's sake? That happen to you? She entice you into a little . . . you know . . . and then whip out the playdough? Famous people sure do lead the life of Sodom and Gomorrah, huh? Lucky we don't turn to salt. You know, even before I made my initial artistic statement of trying to shoot your lights out, I was interested in the creative process. I mean, right this minute, here and now, are you creating? Is it thunderbolts? Is that how the muse strikes you? I'd really like to know.

. . .

I gotta go. Listen, I want to mention that I'll be coming up for parole? If you could put in a good word for me, maybe publicly forgive me, it'd be a help. Maybe our fan clubs could organize something that would be to our mutual benefit. It's been very nice meeting you. Formally, I mean. Don't forget, a word from you would help.

All My Sons

Arthur Miller

Penguin, New York 1974

Act 1

GEORGE:

[*Breathlessly*] My life turned upside down since then. I couldn't go back to work when you left. I wanted to go to Dad and tell him you were going to be married. It seemed impossible not to tell him. He loved you so much. [*He pauses.*] Annie - we did a terrible thing. We can never be forgiven. Not even to send him a card at Christmas. I didn't see him once since I got home from the war! Annie, you don't know what was done to that man. You don't know what happened.

    [ANN [*afraid*]: Of course I know.]

You can't know, you wouldn't be here. Dad came to work that day. The night foreman came to him and showed him the cylinder heads . . . they were coming out of the process with defects. There was something wrong with the process. So Dad went directly to the phone and called here and told Joe to come down right away. But the morning passed. No sign of Joe. So Dad called again. By this time he had over a hundred defectives. The Army was screaming for stuff and Dad didn't have anything to ship. So Joe told him . . . on the phone he told him to weld, cover up the cracks in any way he could, and ship them out.

    [CHRIS: Are you through now?]

[*surging up at him*] I'm not through now! [*Back to* ANN] Dad was afraid. He wanted Joe there if he was going to do it. But Joe can't come down . . . He's sick. Sick! He suddenly gets the flu! Suddenly! But he promised to take responsibility. Do you understand what I'm saying? On the telephone you can't have responsibility! In a court you can always deny a phone call and that's exactly what he did. They knew he was a liar the first time, but in the appeal they believed that rotten lie and now Joe is a big shot and your father is the patsy. [*He gets up.*] Now what're you going to do? Eat his food, sleep in his bed? Answer me; what're you going to do?

Act 3

CHRIS:

I know all about the world. I know the whole crap story. Now listen to this, and tell me what a man's got to be! [*Reads.*] 'My dear Ann: . . .' You listening? He wrote this the day he died. Listen, don't cry, . . . Listen! 'My dear Ann: It is impossible to put down the things I feel. But I've got to tell you something. Yesterday they flew in a load of papers from the States and I read about Dad and your father being convicted. I can't express myself. I can't tell you how I feel – I can't bear to live any more. Last night I circled the base for twenty minutes before I could bring myself in. How could he have done that? Every day three or four men never come back and he sits back there doing business, . . . I don't know how to tell you what I feel, . . . I can't face anybody, . . . I'm going out on a mission in a few minutes. They'll probably report me missing. If they do, I want you to know that you mustn't wait for me. I tell you, Ann, if I had him there now I could kill him – '. [KELLER *grabs letter from* CHRIS's *hand and reads it. After a long pause*] Now blame the world. Do you understand that letter?

223

Nuts

Tom Topper

Samuel French, New York 1981

Act 2

ARTHUR:

We're thinking about a trial. A trial is a public thing, a place where you get shamed in front of the whole world. If she was your daughter, would you put her up there? Would you? [LEVINSKY *shrugs*.] Well, Mister Smartass, she's mine and I'm not going to let a bunch of people, a bunch of stangers, sit in a courtroom and laugh behind their hands at my baby. Oh, no. No, sir. Not while I'm breathing. You're just paid help: the day after tomorrow, you're gone; she's the client to you, and that's all. Well, she's not the client to me. I'm not on her side just because she's giving me a fistful of money. There's 25 years of my love invested in this girl, and I'm not going to sit by and see her shamed in front of the whole goddamn world so you can earn your goddam fee. I know your type. You find scum and you charge 'em an arm and a leg so they can walk around loose. You suck up money from other people's troubles, and you say all you're doing is giving 'em their rights under the law. I know you: whores and killers are your bread and butter. Mister, no child of mine is a whore and a killer. I know what she did, and I know she wasn't in her right mind when she did it. You get that straight.

Loose Ends

Michael Weller   Samuel French, New York 1980

PAUL:

We've always had this kind of an understanding, not like a formal thing. Just we picked it up talking to each other, that it'd be all right if we . . . in theory, that is, in theory it was O.K. If we . . . we weren't like exclusively tied down to each other, you know. If we were attracted to someone . . . and we didn't have to necessarily tell each other if we ever . . . unless we were afraid it was getting out of hand . . . like it was getting too serious and we couldn't handle it. But the thing is, we've never been unfaithful. Unfaithful. Funny how it comes back to words like that. We haven't slept with other people. At least I haven't. And I don't think she has except of course there's no way to know for sure since we said we didn't necessarily have to tell each other. But I really don't think she has. She's probably wanted to. I mean I've wanted to so it stands to reason that she's probably wanted to and the fact that she hasn't, or probably hasn't, uncool though it is to admit it, the fact that there's probably this thing she's wanted to do but didn't do it because she knew how it'd make me feel . . . that always made me feel, like admire her. Not admire exactly. Maybe trust. Respect. Trust. Something like that. Some combination of those things.

 . . . but now that I don't know where she was last night I've been feeling pretty ridiculous, you know. Kind of foolish. Stupid, I don't know what. I was awake all last night thinking about it. I mean, here I am all this time . . . I've known you for what, two years and all that time I've found you like very very attractive, but so what? That's how it goes and now if she's just gone and slept with someone what was all this about? All this holding back for the sake of someone else's feelings . . . and the most ridiculous thing of all is maybe she was in New York thinking you and me were getting it on behind her back and that's what made her . . . if in fact she did do anything, maybe she did it to get even. Or maybe she hasn't done anything. In which case where was she? And why didn't she call? . . .

Do I want to sleep with you?

No, no that's not what I'm saying. I mean, I have wanted to but that's not the point. Primarily. Although I did say it, didn't I? But I always assumed you sort of . . . it was just one of those things. Have you ever thought about it?

PAUL:

Happy birthday. [*Gives* SUSAN *present.*]

I should explain this, by the way. I thought I'd get something really special this year and . . . there's these places midtown you never hear about. At least, I never did. They're shops, right, stores, like they sell things, but. Like where I found this thing. All they sell there is ancient Chinese treasures and you have to make an appointment to even get in the place. So . . . you're inside and you're in a different world. It's completely quiet. You can't hear any sounds from the street and all the stuff is under glass cases like a museum and the lady that shows you around says things like "Now here's an unusual little figurine . . . very rare T'ang Dynasty, perhaps you'd like me to take it out for you." I mean, that's what I call shopping. Do you like it?

Genuine Ming Dynasty. There's only about twenty of them in the world. That's what the lady said. They were only for the royal family. That's why I thought it was a nice idea. What they'd do is if the Emperor had a son that died before he was old enough to rule they'd cremate the body and put the ashes in that hole in the back and then they'd bury the whole works. I guess that's why they're so rare. But listen to this. This is the great part. It's shaped like a horse because they had this belief that the horse would take the child's spirit on a ride where it'd see its whole life passing by . . . the life it would have had if it hadn't died. And that way it could go to its final resting place in peace. At least that's what the lady explained.

But like I said, I wanted to get something really special and I think I got a pretty good deal. They were asking ninety-seven thousand, but I got 'em down to ninety-three. Not bad.

Still, I had to sell the business, all the editing machines, the office equipment, the lease on the building and I had to cash in my stocks and take out all my savings, but I finally scraped it all together.

I just thought it was worth it. We need something in this apartment for all the ashes. The unborn embryos. Isn't that what they do after they take 'em out. Don't they burn 'em, or did you have one of those guys that just pops it in a baggie and into the trash can?

... It's a pretty god damn weird thing to find out about from someone else. That your wife had an abortion six months ago and didn't bother to tell you about it. I guess I must just be one of those naturally curious people because when I found out it made me want to know all kinds of things, Susan. Like just what the fuck has been going on in our life? All these wonderful little human dramas going on under my nose and I didn't know a thing about it. Was it mine?

Moon Children

Michael Weller

New York 1971

BOB:

You want to know something funny, and I mean this really is funny, so you can laugh if you like. There was this lady dying next to my mother and she kept talking about her daughter Susan. Well, Susan came to visit, and you know what? It was only Susan Weinfeld, which doesn't mean anything to you, but she happens to have been the girl I spent a good many of my best months as a sophomore in high school trying to lay. In fact, her virginity almost cost me a B plus in history and here we were, six years later, staring at each other across two dying mothers. I want to tell you something . . . She looked fantastic. And I could tell she was thinking the same thing about me. I mean that kind of scene doesn't happen every day. It was like . . . [*thinks*] . . . it was like how we were the first time. Maybe, just possibly, a little better. So we went out and had a coffee in Mister Donut and started groping each other like crazy under the counter, and I mean we just couldn't keep off each other, so I suggested we get a cab down to my mother's place since, you know, there happened to be no one there at the moment. But the funniest thing was when we get down to Mom's place and you know all those stairs you have to go up and there's Susan all over me practically screaming for it and I start fumbling around with the keys in the lock and none of them would fit. I must've tried every key about fifty fucking times and none of them would fit. Oh, we got in all right. Finally. I had to go downstairs, through the Salvatore's apartment, out the window, up the fire escape, and through Mom's place, but when I opened the front door, guess what? There's poor old Susan asleep on the landing. She really looked cute. I hated to wake her up. Anyway, by the time we'd made coffee and talked and smoked about a million cigarettes each we didn't feel like it anymore. Not really. We did it anyway but, you know, just to be polite, just to make some sense out of evening. It was, taken all in all, a pretty ordinary fuck. The next morning we made plans to meet again that night. We even joked about it, you know, about what a super-fucking good time we'd have, and if you ask me, we could've probably really gotten into something incredible if we'd tried again, but when I went ot the hospital I found out good old Mom had croaked sometime during the night, and somehow, I still don't know why to this day . . . I never got in touch with Susan again. And vice versa. It's a funny thing, you know. At the funeral there were all these people. Friends of Mom's – I didn't know any of them. They were all crying like crazy and I . . . well . . . [*Pause*] I never even got to the burial. The car I was in broke down on the Merritt Parkway. Just as well. I didn't feel like seeing all those people. I'd sure love to have fucked Susan again, though.